THE
FREQUENT
FRYERS
COOKBOOK

How to Deep-Fry Just About Anything That Walks, Crawls, Flies, or Vegetates

THE FREQUENT FRYERS COOKBOOK

RICK BROWNE

ReganBooks
An Imprint of HarperCollinsPublishers

Photographs of Rick Browne by Milan Chuckovich. All other photographs by Rick Browne.

HarperCollins books may be purchased for educational, business, or sales promotional use. For information please write: Special Markets Department, HarperCollins Publishers Inc., 10 East 53rd Street, New York, NY 10022.

FIRST EDITION

Designed by Brenden Hitt

Library of Congress Cataloging-in-Publication Data
    Browne, Rick, 1946–
      The frequent fryers cookbook: how to deep-fry just about anything that walks, crawls, flies, or
         vegetates/Rick Browne.—1st ed.
      p. cm.
      ISBN 0-06-052720-X
      1. Deep frying. I. Title.

    TX689.B76 2003
    641.7'7—dc21

2003041342

03 04 05 06 07   RRD 10 9 8 7 6 5 4 3 2 1

I would like to dedicate this book to four special people:

My mom, Dorothy, for instilling in me the love of good home-cooked food and the fun of cooking it; my dad, Arnold, for instilling in me the love of travel, of going to new places, and of meeting wonderful new people around every bend in the road; my brother Grant, for taking me on hikes and nature walks, thus instilling in me the love of the outdoors, the wonders of nature, and the mystery of all the creatures that inhabit it; and my lovely wife, Kathy, for believing in me, for helping me fulfill a lifelong desire to travel the backroads of America and the world, and for sharing my love of cooking, making new friends, and enjoying life to the fullest.

CONTENTS

INTRODUCTION
FREQUENT FRYERS BEWARE!

Deep-fat frying has been with us almost as long as the discovery that fire would make raw meat taste a whole lot better. In fact, cooking food in various oils or fats is still the only method used in some countries, societies, and single-guy apartments.

And deep-frying in large pots has been practiced in many parts of this country for years. While frying a whole turkey is fairly new to many of us, Southern folks and Texans have been doin' it for decades. "Deep-fried" surely began in a kitchen somewhere in Alabama.

Our aim here is to demystify the process and reveal the culinary delights of this style of cooking. But recently a pall has been spread over the world of deep-frying, spawned by a few vocal, overzealous, and overprotective folks who think those of us who have, or wish to purchase, deep-frying equipment don't have the brains God gave a newt.

Sure, there are safety issues so you won't burn down your garage, deck, or house. But all of those, and I do mean *all*, can be addressed and dismissed with a liberal application of what we Americans are best known for (in most cases anyway): *common sense*.

Add some frying recipes and some helpful hints and techniques offered up here, and there should be *no* problem deep-frying that turkey, roast, game hen, prawn, or doughnut. Using a propane burner without proper preparation to boil several gallons of oil can be hazardous. But following the manufacturer's suggestions, having the good sense to pick up and read this book, and using your brain as something other than to hold your ears apart will ensure a safe, fun, and delicious experience as a frequent fryer!

P-FRYING BASICS

DEEP-FRYING
BASICS

DEEP-FRYING TIPS

- Maintain a frying temperature of at least 350 degrees F (175 degrees C). That way the battered, breaded surfaces will quickly form a protective shield, keeping the oil from penetrating the food as it cools, and keeping it virtually grease-free.

- *Do not salt food* before deep-frying. Salt draws moisture to the surface, which can splatter when the food is added to the hot oil. Salt also lowers the smoke point and breaks down the oil more quickly. Only add salt, if at all, just before eating.

- Dip the food in lightly beaten egg and then roll it in seasoned bread crumbs. Allow the uncooked breaded food to rest on a rack at room temperature for 15 to 20 minutes before frying so that the food can partially dry and the crumbs adhere to the food.

- Have the eggs at room temperature and avoid beating them too much. Air bubbles in overwhisked eggs form pockets on the food when it's dipped into the egg. These pockets won't retain the breading.

- If the oil is too hot, the coating will burn from the intense heat of the oil before the food inside the batter/coating has had time to cook properly. Burned outside, and semi-raw inside. Not a good thing!

- Don't jam the fryer with food. Things need space to cook right, and too much food will lower the oil's temperature.

- Small bread crumbs adhere to food much better than large bread crumbs.

- For each portion of food, use at least six times as much oil.

- Heat the oil to 15 degrees F (7 to 8 degrees C) higher than its optimal deep-frying temperature. This is to allow for the immediate cooling of the oil when food is added. Preheating it higher than this may damage the oil's molecular structure.

RECOMMENDED FRYING AND DEEP-FRYING OILS

DEEP FRY

Peanut oil is good if you want to fry repeatedly with the same oil, but it should be used only for a few hours per day.

Sunflower oil can be used if you fry the whole day continuously with the same oil. But after this one day of extensive use, it might have to be replaced. .

SHALLOW FRY

Coconut fat is good for frying if it is not hydrogenated (hardened). Hydrogenated fats and oils are extremely dangerous for your health and should be omitted from a healthful diet because they contain harmful transfatty acids.

Clarified butter is very good for frying but it is more expensive than most oils.

Olive oil contains many monounsaturated fatty acids and is good for pan frying but not for the rigors of extensive deep-frying.

Canola oil made from rapeseed is used extensively in food service. You can use it at home, but peanut oil is the oil of choice for home frying.

The flavor these oils add to the cooked food is minimal, so it's up to you which you use.

HOW MUCH OIL DO I NEED?

The size of the pot you're cooking in determines the amount of oil you need. The majority of recipes in this book are intended for cooking in a *deep pot fryer*, which is large enough for whole turkeys, but of course can be used for smaller items. To determine how much oil is needed for cooking in your deep pot fryer, use the following guidelines.

Water displacement method You should *always* use this method to pre-measure the oil for turkeys or other fowl, roasts, and large fish. This method will keep you from over-filling or underfilling the fryer with oil.

1. Put what you want to cook in the pot (unmarinated and unbreaded) and add water until it covers the food by about 2 inches.

2. Remove the food, and then measure and mark the new water level with a pencil (they're graphite, not lead, these days, so you're safe!).

3. Drain the pot, dry it, and then add the correct amount of oil.

4. After you remove the food from the water, remember that you must thoroughly dry it, since any water left can be dangerous when it makes contact with the hot oil.

Most of the time when you use a deep pot fryer, and for most of the recipes in this book, 2 to 5 gallons of oil will be necessary. Due to differences in size, however, it's important to use the water displacement method to be sure.

- *For large batches* or volumes of food, but not necessarily as large as whole fowl or roasts, you will usually need about 6 inches of oil in the fryer. French fries are an example that falls under this category.

- *For small batches* or volumes of food, you will probably need less oil—about 4 inches of oil should be enough.

- Maintain an oil temperature of at least 350 degrees F, but no higher than 400 degrees F.

Some of the recipes in this book can also be accomplished in a large Dutch oven, which requires much less oil. A good guideline to use is 2 to 3 inches of oil in these cooking pots. But, as with the deep pot fryer, be careful not to overfill them with oil or food, to prevent the oil from overflowing and igniting on the gas flame. As you know, you don't want to crowd the pot, so each item will have enough space to cook.

SMOKE POINTS OF OILS

Knowing the smoke point of the oil you intend to cook with is important because each time you deep-fry, you lower its smoke point irreversibly. The smoke point is the temperature when the oil begins to break down and smoke. When the oil breaks down it is unusable for cooking.

If your oil's smoke point is just above 350 to 375 degrees F (175 to 190 degrees C), which is the normal deep-frying temperature, chances are its smoke point will drop below 375 degrees F (190 degrees C) after its first use, rendering it useless for further deep-frying.

If you want to save money by reusing an oil as many times as possible, select one with a high smoke point.

FACTORS THAT WILL DECREASE THE SMOKE POINT OF ANY OIL:

- combination of vegetable oils in products
- foreign properties in oil (crumbs from batter)
- temperature to which oil is heated
- presence of salt
- number of times oil is used
- length of time oil is heated
- exposure to oxygen and light during storage
- temperature at which oil is stored

OIL SMOKE POINTS

Oil	Temperature Celsius / Fahrenheit
Safflower	265° / 509°
Sunflower	246° / 475°
Soybean	241° / 465°
Canola	238° / 460°
Corn	236° / 457°
Peanut	231° / 448°
Sesame	215° / 419°
Olive	190° / 374°

Don't heat the oil above the smoke point. Not only does the oil start to break down at this point, but it is also getting too close to the flash and fire points, and this can be extremely dangerous.

An oil reaches its *flash point* (about 600 degrees F [320 degrees C] for most oils) when tiny wisps of fire begin to leap from its surface. You do not want to get to this point.

If the oil is heated to its *fire point* (slightly under 700 degrees F [400 degrees C] for most oils), its surface will be ablaze, and you have a big problem at hand. See Safety Precautions (page 11) for fire-extinguishing methods.

TIME AND TEMPERATURE GUIDELINES FOR DEEP-FRYING

VEGETABLES

Item	Temperature	Frying Time
French fries, raw	360°F	5 to 6 minutes
French fries, frozen	360°F	4 to 5 minutes
French fries, frozen, blanched	360°F	3 to 4 minutes
Onion rings, breaded, fresh	360°F	3 to 4 minutes
Onion rings, breaded, frozen	360°F	4 to 5 minutes
Vegetables, assorted, breaded	360°F	5 to 6 minutes
Vegetable fritters	360°F	6 to 8 minutes

SEAFOOD

Item	Temperature	Frying Time
Clam strips, breaded, fresh	360°F	1.5 minutes
Clam strips, breaded, frozen	360°F	2 to 3 minutes
Fish fillet, breaded, fresh	360°F	3 to 4 minutes
Fish fillet, breaded, frozen	360°F	4 to 5 minutes
Oysters, breaded	360°F	3 to 4 minutes
Scallops, breaded, fresh, large	360°F	2 to 3 minutes
Scallops, breaded, frozen, large	360°F	4 minutes
Shrimp, breaded, fresh	360°F	3 to 4 minutes
Shrimp, breaded, frozen	360°F	4 to 5 minutes

BREADED MEATS

Item	Temperature	Frying Time
Chicken pieces, breaded, frozen or fresh	360°F	5 to 6 minutes
Chicken, whole, breaded, large	360°F	10 to 14 minutes
Chicken, whole, breaded, small	360°F	8 to 12 minutes
Cutlet, breaded, frozen or fresh	360°F	5 to 6 minutes

SWEETS AND FRUITS

Item	Temperature	Frying Time
Cake doughnuts	375°F	2 to 2.5 minutes
Fruit-filled fritters	360°F	5 to 7 minutes
Yeast-raised doughnuts	375°F	3 minutes
Plums, cherries, peaches, apples, and so on	350°F	30 seconds to 1 minute

DEEP-FRYING WITHOUT A THERMOMETER

If you do not have a thermometer but want to deep-fry, this method is a last resort to get approximate temperatures of oil. Here are the temperatures and times at which a 1-inch cube of white bread will turn golden brown:

345°–355°F	65 seconds
355°–365°F	60 seconds
365°–375°F	50 seconds
375°–385°F	40 seconds
385°–395°F	20 seconds
395°–400°F	10 seconds

PROLONGING OIL'S USEFUL LIFE

- The longer an oil is heated, the more quickly it will decompose, so avoid preheating the oil any longer than necessary. If you're frying more than one batch of anything, quickly add each new batch, unless you need more time to bring the temperature back up. Turn off the heat as soon as you're finished cooking.

- The hotter oil gets, the faster it begins to decompose and fail. So don't cook at 375 degrees F if your recipe suggests 325 degrees F.

- Use a *quality* deep-fat frying thermometer.

- Shake off loose bread crumbs from breaded food before cooking. Crumbs and other particles scorch quickly and will speed up the demise of your oil. Use a small strainer, a strainer lined with a paper towel, or a slotted spoon to remove as many crumbs as you can.

- Do not mix used oil with fresh oil.

- When the oil has cooled enough that it is safe to handle, strain it through paper towels, coffee filters, or cheesecloth (or two of these in succession) into its original empty container or a clear glass jar.

- If food particles are not filtered out frequently, they tend to burn and cause the oil not only to fail more quickly, but they can also form toxic chemicals in the oil. Filter after each use when you pour the oil back into its storage container. That's right, filter deep-fat fryer oil *every* time you use it!

- The longer you use oil, the more it starts to oxidize and deteriorate. So between frying sessions, store the oil, tightly sealed, in a cool, dark place or in the refrigerator. The oil may cloud in the refrigerator, but it will become clear again at room temperature. Storing the oil this way will help prolong its life.

TIME TO CHANGE THE OIL?

- Oil darkens with use because the oil itself, and tiny food particles in it, burn when put to a high heat.

- The more you use an oil, the more slowly it will pour. Its viscosity changes because of changes to the oil's molecular structure. When it pours like ketchup, throw it out!

- Loose food particles collect as sediment at the bottom of the container you're storing oil in, or float in the oil.

- When smoke appears on the surface of the oil, before the temperature reaches 375 degrees F (190 degrees C), your oil is no good.

- If the oil has a rancid smell or if it smells like the foods you've cooked in it, throw it away. There's nothing worse than cooking a turkey in fishy smelling oil, or vice versa.

SAFETY PRECAUTIONS

- *Never* use water to put out an oil fire: the water will splatter the burning oil and spread it more quickly.

- Instead, smother the flames with a tight-fitting lid or sheet of aluminum foil.

- If the fire has spread outside the pan, suffocate it with baking soda or an ABC fire extinguisher formulated for oil fires.

- *Never* leave your fryer unattended.

- Eating foods cooked in oxidized or spoiled oils can cause major stomach distress. Please refer to Time to Change the Oil? (pages 9–10) for when oil should no longer be used.

NO. 1
APPETIZERS

NO. 1

APPETIZERS

ACADIAN POPCORN

2 pounds raw crawfish tails
   (or small shrimp)

2 large eggs

1 cup dry white wine

½ cup cornmeal

½ cup flour

1 tablespoon chopped fresh chives

1 clove garlic, minced

½ teaspoon dried thyme

½ teaspoon chervil

¼ teaspoon garlic salt

¼ teaspoon black pepper

¼ teaspoon cayenne pepper

¼ teaspoon paprika

Oil for frying

Rinse the crawfish or shrimp in cold water, drain well, and refrigerate until needed. Whisk the eggs and wine in a small bowl. In another small bowl, combine the cornmeal, flour, chives, garlic, thyme, chervil, salt, pepper, cayenne pepper, and paprika. Gradually whisk the dry ingredients into the egg mixture, blending well. Cover the resulting batter and then let it stand for 1 to 2 hours at room temperature.

Heat the oil in a Dutch oven or deep fryer to 375 degrees F.

Dip the dry seafood into the batter and fry it in small batches for 2 to 3 minutes, turning it until golden brown throughout.

Remove the crawfish (or shrimp) with a slotted spoon and thoroughly drain it on several layers of paper towels. Serve it on a heated platter with your favorite dip.

SERVES 4 TO 6

BOB'S BEER-BATTERED ONION RINGS

3 large yellow onions
2 cups whole milk, chilled
2 cups ice water

BATTER

1⅓ cups flour
1 teaspoon salt
1 teaspoon dry mustard
¼ teaspoon freshly ground pepper
2 large eggs, at room temperature
2 tablespoons vegetable oil
¾ cup beer, at room temperature
Dash of hot sauce

Oil for frying

On the night before cooking, slice the onions crosswise about ½ inch thick and then carefully separate the slices into rings. (You should have about 8 cups.) Place the rings in a wide, shallow dish in as few layers as possible.

In a bowl, whisk together the milk and ice water. Pour the mixture over the onions. Cover the dish with plastic wrap and refrigerate overnight. Turn the rings at least once to soak them evenly.

In a large bowl, whisk together the flour, salt, mustard, and pepper. In a medium bowl, lightly beat the eggs; whisk in the vegetable oil, and then the beer and hot sauce, mixing well. Make a well in the center of the flour mixture and pour in the egg mixture all at once. Whisk until the mixture is free of lumps. Cover and let it stand overnight.

The next day, cover two large cookie sheets with a double layer of paper towels. Using tongs, remove the onion rings from the milk mixture, shaking off the excess liquid, and let the rings drain on the towels. Pat the rings dry to remove all excess moisture.

Heat the oil in a deep fryer to 375 degrees F.

Stir the batter and, working in batches, use the tongs to dip the onion rings in the batter, shaking off any excess. Quickly slide them into the hot oil. Fry the rings, turning occasionally, until they are a deep golden brown on both sides. This will take 4 to 5 minutes. Transfer the cooked onion rings from the oil to another paper-towel-lined cookie sheet. Let them drain briefly, then serve while quite hot.

SERVES 6

FRENCH POTATO CURLS

4 pounds potatoes

Salt, garlic salt,
    or celery salt to taste

¼ cup grated Parmesan cheese

Oil for frying

Scrub the potatoes thoroughly with a vegetable brush. Using a potato peeler, cut off long spirals of skin from the potatoes. In a large saucepan, cover the skins with very cold water and let them stand 30 minutes to 1 hour. Save the peeled potatoes in cold water and use them for another dish of your choice. Drain and carefully pat the curls dry with paper towels.

Heat the oil in a deep fryer to 375 degrees F. Using tongs, drop the curls into the hot oil and fry them until golden brown and crisp, about 1 minute.

Using tongs, remove them from the fryer and drain on paper towels. Sprinkle them with salt, garlic salt, or celery salt, and Parmesan cheese. Serve hot.

SERVES 4 TO 6

FRICKLES (FRIED PICKLES)

1 cup flour

1 cup yellow cornmeal

2 tablespoons your favorite
    BBQ rub

¼ cup prepared yellow mustard

2 tablespoons beer

Dill pickle slices

Oil for frying

Heat the oil in a deep fryer to 350 degrees F.

In a wide flat pan, combine the flour and cornmeal and season the mixture with the BBQ rub. In a small bowl make a slurry of mustard and beer.

Using your fingers, dip the pickle slices in the mustard mixture and then in the flour/cornmeal. Then, using tongs, slip individual pickle slices into the hot oil. Deep-fry until the batter is browned. The pickles will float to the top of the oil when done.

Remove them from the hot oil with tongs and drain them on paper towels on a shallow plate.

Serve these as an appetizer with an icy cold beer.

SERVES 6 TO 8

"FRYED" ONION BLOSSOMS

IF THERE IS A "SOLD ONLY ON TV" STORE IN A MALL NEAR YOU, GO AND BUY THE ONION BLOSSOM CUTTER. IT WORKS GREAT AND IS A LOT LESS WORK THAN DOING EACH CUT BY HAND.

DIP

½ cup mayonnaise

½ cup sour cream

2 tablespoons ketchup

1 tablespoon chili powder

1½ teaspoons McCormick Cajun
    seasoning

1 or 2 large sweet onions

BREADING

1¼ cups flour

1 tablespoon McCormick Cajun
    seasoning

1 cup milk

Oil for frying

In a small bowl, make the dip by combining mayonnaise, sour cream, ketchup, chili powder, and 1½ teaspoons Cajun seasoning. Mix well and set aside.

Heat the oil in a deep fryer to 350 degrees F.

Leaving the root end intact, peel the outer skin of the onion. Cut a small slice off the top. Starting at the top of the onion and on one side, make a cut downward toward the root end, stopping ½ inch from the bottom. Make additional cuts ⅛ inch from the first cut until there are cuts completely across the top of the onion. Turn the onion a quarter turn so the slices are horizontal to you. Repeat the cuts ⅛ inch apart from each other until there is a checkerboard pattern across the entire top of the onion.

In a large bowl or resealable plastic bag, combine the flour and 1 tablespoon Cajun seasoning. Pour the milk into a small bowl. Dip the onion in flour, then dip it into the milk, then back into the flour mixture. Fry the onion in the hot oil for 5 minutes or until golden, turning once.

Using tongs, remove the onion from the oil and drain on paper towels. Place it on a serving plate. With a spoon, remove the center of the fried onion blossom. Pour about ½ cup of the dip into the center of the blossom and serve it immediately.

SERVES 4 TO 6

GREEN DRAGONS WITH A GOLDEN HEART

1 (8-ounce) bottle of Velveeta
   cheese spread (see Note)

2 cups whole jalapeño peppers

1 cup flour

1 teaspoon salt

1 teaspoon sugar

1 teaspoon ground black
   pepper

1 teaspoon chili powder

1 teaspoon garlic powder

2 eggs

1 cup beer

Oil for frying

Put the contents of the bottle of Velveeta in a cloth pastry bag. Place the bag in a microwave and heat on medium heat for 1 to 1½ minutes until the cheese is very soft and runny. Set it aside.

Cut a slit the entire length of each jalapeño and gently spread it apart. Take your pastry bag of warmed cheese and fill the inside of each jalapeño with cheese. Use just enough to fill the inside, being careful that the edges of the cut don't gap.

Mix the flour, salt, sugar, black pepper, chili powder, garlic powder, eggs, and beer together in a bowl. It should be quite thick. You may have to adjust by adding more flour to make a very thick paste that sticks to the pepper.

Heat the oil in a deep fryer or large pot to 365 degrees F.

Dip the stuffed jalapeños in the batter, and drain quickly. Using long tongs, place them immediately into the deep fryer. Cook the jalapeños until they float to the surface of the oil, 1 to 2 minutes. They should be golden brown and crispy. Remove the jalapeños from the hot oil using tongs, drain them on paper towels, and serve them immediately.

SERVES 4 TO 6

Note: Instead of Velveeta, you can use cream cheese to which you've added yellow food coloring to make the filling a deep orange color.

KOH SAMUI SPRING ROLLS

½ pound ground pork (or chicken)

1 tablespoon rice wine

1½ teaspoons arrowroot

¼ teaspoon black pepper

1 tablespoon sugar

1 tablespoon soy sauce

2 tablespoons vegetable oil

1 tablespoon salt

2 tablespoons minced fresh ginger

1 clove garlic, finely minced

1 cup chopped onion

1½ pounds chopped Chinese cabbage (bok choy)

1 pound fresh bean sprouts

2 packages spring roll skins

1 egg, beaten

Oil for frying

Mix the pork or chicken with the wine, arrowroot, pepper, sugar, and soy sauce in a large bowl and set aside. Put the vegetable oil in a medium saucepan over high heat, and add the pork or chicken mixture. Cook until all the pink color is gone, 10 to 15 minutes. Add the salt, ginger, garlic, and onion; cook for 3 to 4 minutes.

Remove the mixture from the heat and drain in a colander for 5 minutes, saving the liquid, then spread the mixture on a cookie sheet to cool completely. Pour the reserved liquid into a pan and add the cabbage. Cook it for 5 minutes over high heat, then remove from the heat, add the bean sprouts, and drain well in the colander. Add the pork or chicken mixture and stir well. Salt and pepper to taste.

Heat the frying oil in a deep fryer to 360 degrees F.

To assemble the spring rolls, lay one spring roll skin on a cutting board with the point of the skin facing toward you. Place ⅓ cup of the filling on the skin and roll it up, folding the edges toward the middle. To seal the end, brush it with the beaten egg.

When all the rolls are assembled, put them in the deep fryer in small batches and fry until golden brown, 3 to 5 minutes. Serve with hoisin or plum sauce.

SERVES 6 TO 8

LES JAMBES FRITES DE GRENOUILLE (YOU KNOW, D'EM FROGS' LEGS)

BREADING

½ cup flour

¼ cup seasoned bread crumbs

½ teaspoon lemon pepper

¼ teaspoon garlic powder

½ teaspoon green onion powder

½ teaspoon summer savory

Dash of Louisiana hot sauce

1 teaspoon seasoned salt

BATTER

4 large eggs

½ cup milk or beer

⅓ cup blush wine, like Zinfandel

2 cups flour

¼ cup seasoned bread crumbs

1 teaspoon garlic salt

¼ teaspoon ground cumin

½ teaspoon onion powder

1 teaspoon Louisiana hot sauce

1½ to 2 pounds frogs' legs

1 cup flour

Oil for frying

In a large bowl, whisk together the breading ingredients to mix thoroughly. Set aside.

Using another large bowl, whisk together the batter ingredients until the batter is smooth and all the ingredients are well incorporated.

Heat oil in a deep fryer to 375 degrees F.

Wash the frogs' legs thoroughly. Put the flour in a wide flat pan. Dip each leg into the pan of flour, rolling them so they have a light coating of flour. Then take each leg and dip it into the batter. After briefly draining, dip the leg into the breading and again roll so it's well covered with dry coating. Set on a plate while you finish with the rest of the legs.

Once you have finished coating all the legs, slip them (6 or 8 at a time) into the hot oil and fry till brown on all sides, about 3 minutes.

Remove the legs from the oil with a slotted spoon or tongs and drain them briefly on paper towels. Serve on a heated platter over dirty rice.

SERVES 2 TO 4

MICKEY'S MOZZARELLA LOGS

1 pound mozzarella cheese

1 cup flour

⅓ cup cornstarch

3 eggs, beaten

¼ cup white wine

1½ cups Italian bread crumbs

1 teaspoon granulated garlic

½ teaspoon dried savory

½ teaspoon dried basil

Pinch red pepper

Parmesan cheese for sprinkling

Oil for frying

Heat the oil in a deep pot or Dutch oven to 350 degrees F.

Slice the mozzarella lengthwise into ½-inch sections. Then cut each section in half so you have strips 3 to 4 inches long by ½ inch wide.

In a medium bowl, mix the flour with the cornstarch and set the bowl aside. In another medium bowl, beat the eggs with a hand beater or whisk, add the white wine, whisk until incorporated, and set aside.

In a flat pan or bowl, mix the bread crumbs, garlic, savory, basil, and red pepper, and set aside.

Roll the cheese logs in the flour, then dip in the egg-wine mixture, and then roll the logs in the bread crumb mixture.

Using tongs or a slotted spatula, carefully slip the logs (2 or 3 at a time) into the hot oil and fry them until golden brown. This will take only a few seconds, so you need to watch them closely.

Remove the logs with a spatula or tongs and drain them on paper towels. Sprinkle with Parmesan cheese. Serve them with marinara sauce or ranch dressing to dip.

SERVES 8

N'ORLEANS SHRIMP CROQUETTES

1 pound shrimp

2 thin slices fresh ginger

1 clove garlic

1 large stalk celery, very crisp

1 teaspoon soy sauce

1 tablespoon oyster sauce

1 teaspoon fish sauce

3 tablespoons chicken broth

2 tablespoons cornstarch

1 teaspoon salt

Lettuce leaves for garnish

Oil for frying

Heat the oil in a deep fryer to 350 degrees F.

Clean and devein the shrimp. Chop the shrimp very fine, almost into a paste. Mince the ginger and garlic and keep them separate from the shrimp. Slice the celery into ¼-inch pieces, removing strings as you cut.

In a small bowl, whisk together the soy sauce, oyster sauce, fish sauce, chicken broth, and 1 tablespoon of the cornstarch, and set aside.

In another bowl, combine the shrimp with half of the minced ginger and half of the minced garlic. Add the salt and the remaining 1 tablespoon of cornstarch. Mix well, and with lightly moistened hands form this mixture into small croquettes about 2 inches long and 1 inch in diameter.

Preheat the oven to 200 degrees F.

Deep-fry the shrimp croquettes 6 at a time, until they are golden brown, 2 to 3 minutes. Remove the croquettes from the hot oil with tongs.

Drain the croquettes on paper towels and keep them warm on a platter in the oven.

Put 1 tablespoon of the hot oil from the deep-fry pan in a saucepan or wok over high heat and stir-fry the remaining ginger and garlic until it turns golden, about 1 minute. Add the celery and stir-fry it on high heat for about 30 seconds. Add the reserved sauce mixture and stir until it thickens, 2 to 3 minutes.

Cover a platter with lettuce leaves and arrange the croquettes on the leaves. Remove the sauce from the heat and pour it over the croquettes. Serve hot.

SERVES 8

SI SI CINNAMON SINNERS

ANNE CALLON OF JALISCO, MEXICO, SAYS THESE ARE A FAVORITE WAY TO SPEND A STORMY EVENING DURING THE WINTER.

SPICE MIX

1 cup sugar

1 teaspoon ground cinnamon

¼ teaspoon ground nutmeg

¼ teaspoon ground allspice

10 (8-inch) flour tortillas

Oil for frying

Heat the oil in a deep fryer to 375 degrees F.

In a large paper bag, combine the sugar, cinnamon, nutmeg, and allspice, and set aside. Cut the tortillas into 2- × 3-inch strips.

Slip 4 to 5 strips into the hot oil at a time and fry them until golden brown on both sides, about 30 seconds per side. With a slotted spoon remove the strips, and drain them on paper towels.

While the strips are still warm, place them in the paper bag with the sugar-spice mixture and shake gently to coat the strips evenly.

Remove the strips to a large bowl and serve immediately. Or you may store them in an air-tight container and serve cold.

SERVES 6 TO 8

SUGARED WALNUTS

3 cups water

2 cups walnuts, in large pieces
   (or pecans)

¼ cup firmly packed brown sugar

Salt to taste

1 tablespoon granulated sugar

¼ teaspoon ground cinnamon

Oil for frying

Bring the water to a rolling boil in a large saucepan. Add the walnuts and blanch (boil) them for 1 minute. Remove from the heat, rinse the nuts under hot water, and briefly drain them. Then, in a small bowl, toss the walnuts with the brown sugar.

Heat the oil in a Dutch oven to 350 degrees F.

With a slotted spoon, add half the walnuts to the oil. Fry, stirring constantly, 4 to 5 minutes or until golden. Repeat with the remaining nuts. Sprinkle with salt, granulated sugar, and cinnamon and stir together.

Separate the pieces and cool them on an aluminum foil sheet. Serve warm.

SERVES 4

LA BELLA LUNA FRIED RAVIOLI

SERVE THESE GOLDEN TREATS WITH YOUR FAVORITE MARINARA OR TOMATO SAUCE FOR DIPPING.

2 eggs

½ cup heavy cream

3 cups seasoned bread crumbs

¼ cup grated Parmesan cheese

1 tablespoon granulated garlic

1 tablespoon oregano

Pinch of salt

2 pounds frozen ravioli (beef or cheese)

Fresh parsley sprigs for garnish

Oil for frying

Preheat the oil in a deep fryer to 365 degrees F. Preheat an oven to 200 degrees F.

In a wide, flat bowl, with a wire whisk, beat the eggs and cream together until frothy. In a medium bowl, combine the bread crumbs, cheese, garlic, oregano, and salt.

Dip the frozen raviolis (4 or 5 at a time) into the egg mixture and then into the bread crumbs, coating each ravioli well.

In small batches (4 or 5 at a time), slip the ravioli into the hot oil and cook until they are golden brown, about 3 minutes. Remove from the hot oil with a slotted spoon or frying basket and drain on paper towels. Place the raviolis on a plate in the warmed oven until the rest are done.

Serve on a heated platter garnished with fresh parsley springs, accompanied by bowls of dipping sauce.

SERVES 4 TO 6

COUCH POTATO SKINS

4 large baking potatoes

1 teaspoon garlic salt

¼ teaspoon cayenne pepper

1 teaspoon dried sage

Sour cream for topping

Chopped chives or green
**   onions for topping**

Shredded Cheddar cheese
**   for topping**

Oil for frying

Preheat the oven to 400 degrees F.

Wash and dry the potatoes. Bake them for 1 hour, or until tender.

Preheat the oil in a deep fryer to 375 degrees F.

When the potatoes are cool enough to be handled with bare hands, in 15 to 20 minutes, cut them in half lengthwise and scoop out most of the soft potato insides. Reserve to make potato salad or potato pancakes.

Cut each potato half in quarters lengthwise. Refrigerate the skins for 1 to 2 hours.

Mix the garlic salt, pepper, and sage in a shaker and set aside.

Using a fryer basket or a large slotted spoon, lower the potato quarters into the hot oil and cook until crisp and browned, in 2 to 3 minutes. Remove skins from the hot oil and drain them on paper towels. Sprinkle each with the spice mixture. Serve with the sour cream, chives, and shredded cheese on the side.

Enjoy the game, sport!

SERVES 4 TO 6

MELBUNN MIKEY'S WINGS

MARINADE

¼ cup soy sauce

¼ cup cheap, very cheap, beer

¼ cup oyster sauce

1 teaspoon Vietnamese fish sauce

1 teaspoon Louisiana hot sauce (or
  your favorite hot sauce)

2 pounds chicken wings

COATING

1 cup flour

1 cup cornmeal

1 teaspoon cayenne pepper

1 teaspoon granulated garlic

1 teaspoon salt

1 teaspoon white pepper

Oil for frying

Ranch dressing, chilled, for dipping

Celery sticks for garnish

In a medium bowl, combine the marinade ingredients and whisk until well mixed.

Clean the chicken wings, drain them, and place them in a 1-quart Ziploc plastic bag. Pour the marinade into the bag to cover the wings. Place the bag in a bowl in the refrigerator and marinate for at least 12 hours.

Remove the wings from the marinade, discarding the liquid. Preheat the deep-frying oil to 375 degrees F.

In a wide, shallow bowl, mix the coating ingredients. Add the wings, turning them until they are well-coated.

With a slotted spoon or frying basket, slip 4 to 5 wings at a time into the hot oil and fry until golden brown, 4 to 5 minutes. Remove the wings from the oil and drain on paper towels.

Serve with good Aussie beer or Yank brew if you haven't any "down under" beverages handy. Have chilled ranch dressing and celery sticks on hand to assuage the temperature created by the hot wings.

SERVES 4

JALISCO JALAPEÑO FRY

1 cup flour

1 teaspoon granulated garlic

1 teaspoon Mexene chili
    powder (or your favorite
    chili powder)

1 teaspoon salt

½ teaspoon white pepper

¼ teaspoon cayenne pepper

2 eggs, beaten

8 ounces beer, dark or light

¼ cup water

2 cups jalapeño peppers

Oil for frying

Preheat the oil in a deep fryer to 365 degrees F.

In a wide, shallow bowl, combine the flour, garlic, chili powder, salt, white pepper, and cayenne pepper. Mix well. Add the eggs, beer, and water and stir the batter until smooth.

Cut the jalapeños into 1-inch slices and dip each slice into the batter, coating them well. Using a bamboo or metal skewer, slip the jalapeño rings into the hot oil and fry until they float to the surface and begin to brown, 2 to 3 minutes.

Remove the rings from the hot oil, drain on paper towels, and serve.

SERVES 6 TO 8

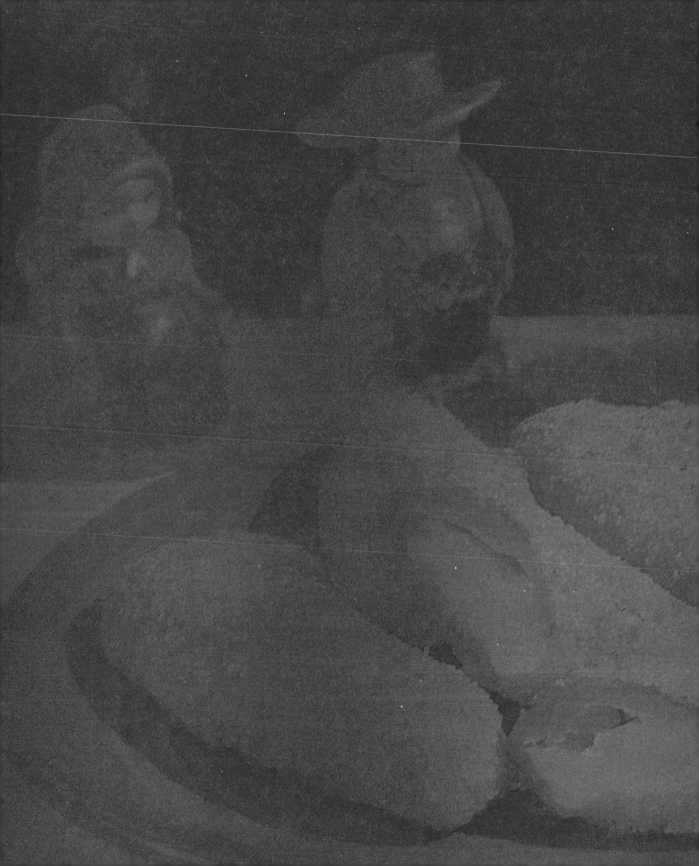

NO. 2

BREADS PASTRIES

NO. 2

BREADS & PASTRIES

BENGALI FRIED DOUGH WAFERS

1¼ cups all-purpose flour

1¼ cups whole wheat flour

1 teaspoon salt

1 teaspoon black pepper

1 cup ice water

Oil for frying

In a deep bowl, combine the all-purpose and whole wheat flours, add salt and pepper, and stir the ingredients with a fork to mix them well. Make a depression in the center and add the ice water while stirring with the fork. If the mixture gets too dry, add more ice water, a teaspoon at a time. Stir until the dough clings together but isn't sticky.

Place the dough on a floured board and knead it for 5 minutes. Form it into a ball. Cut the ball in quarters, then cut each of those quarters into 3 pieces. On a floured surface form the dough into small balls, place them on a plate, cover, and let them rest for 30 to 40 minutes.

Heat the oil in a deep fryer or Dutch oven to 375 degrees F.

On a piece of floured wax paper, roll out each ball into wafer-thin rounds 6 to 7 inches in diameter. Place them in a single layer on the wax paper, putting sheets of paper between each round (otherwise, they'll stick together).

Gently slip each flour wafer into the hot oil. First it will sink and then it will rise to the top of the hot oil. When it rises back to the surface, use a wooden spoon or long tongs and hold the wafer under the surface until it puffs, about 20 seconds on each side until puffed and golden brown. Using tongs or a spatula, remove the wafers from the heat and drain on paper towels.

Serve with beans, curry dishes, or salsa dishes.

SERVES 6 TO 8

BUTTERMILK 'N BACON HUSH PUPPIES

2 cups yellow cornmeal

1 cup flour

¾ cup white or yellow corn
   (if using frozen, thaw
   completely)

¾ teaspoon seasoned salt

½ teaspoon ground pepper

1 teaspoon baking powder

1 teaspoon baking soda

2 tablespoons brown sugar

2 eggs

2 tablespoons bacon
   grease, melted

1 cup buttermilk

Oil for frying

Mix the cornmeal, flour, corn, salt, pepper, baking powder, baking soda, and brown sugar in a medium bowl. Add the eggs, bacon grease, and buttermilk. Stir until the ingredients are thoroughly blended. Flour your hands and using approximately 2 tablespoons of the thick batter, roll the hush puppies into small balls, 1 to 1½ inches in diameter.

Heat the oil in a deep fryer to 350 degrees F. Drop the hush puppies in the oil using a tablespoon. Allow them to brown on all sides, 2 to 3 minutes.

They should begin floating when done, but if they don't, don't overcook them. They're ready when they're golden brown all over. Remove them from the oil with a slotted spoon or tongs, drain on paper towels, and serve immediately.

SERVES 6 TO 8

FRY D'AT BREAD, MOMMA

3 cups flour

2 teaspoons baking powder

1 teaspoon salt

¾ to 1 cup warm buttermilk

2 tablespoons butter or
**   margarine, melted**

1 teaspoon sugar

Oil for frying

In a large bowl, mix the flour, baking powder, and salt thoroughly. Add enough warm buttermilk to make a soft, easy-to-knead dough. Knead on a floured board until the dough is very smooth and soft, but still elastic. Divide the dough into 6 to 8 balls and brush the tops with the melted butter. Cover the balls and let stand 35 to 45 minutes.

Heat the oil in a deep fryer to 375 degrees F.

Pat out each ball into a round, 5 or 6 inches in diameter and ¼ inch thick. Fry dough rounds in the hot oil until they rise to the surface, almost immediately. Then cook them until they are light brown on one side. Turn with a large spoon or spatula and brown them on the other side. Do not pierce the crust.

Remove the cooked bread from the hot oil with a slotted spoon and drain on paper towels. Sprinkle with the sugar. Serve hot.

SERVES 6 TO 8

GRAND MARNIER BEIGNETS

1 (¼-ounce) packet dry yeast

4 tablespoons warm water

3½ cups flour

1 teaspoon salt

¼ cup sugar

1 teaspoon orange granules
   (see Note)

1 cup plus 2 tablespoons
   milk

3 eggs, beaten

¼ cup butter, melted

2 tablespoons Grand Marnier
   (orange liqueur)

1 cup confectioners' sugar

¼ cup lemon juice (optional)

Oil for frying

In a small bowl dissolve the yeast in the warm water. Set the bowl aside in a warm place for 15 to 20 minutes.

In a large mixing bowl, combine the flour, salt, sugar, and orange granules, and mix well to ensure proper blending. Fold in the dissolved yeast, the milk, eggs, butter, and liqueur. Continue to blend until a smooth dough is formed. Place the dough in a medium bowl, cover it with a damp towel, and allow the dough to rise for 1 hour.

Remove the dough to a well-floured surface and roll it out to approximately ¼-inch thickness. Cut it into rectangular shapes, 2 × 3 inches, and return them to a lightly floured pan. Cover the pan with a towel and allow the dough to rise for 35 to 45 minutes.

Heat the oil in a deep fryer to 375 degrees F.

Deep-fry the squares in the hot oil, turning once, until golden brown, 3 to 4 minutes. Remove from the oil with a slotted spoon or basket strainer. Drain the beignets on a paper towel, and then dust generously with confectioners' sugar. If you like, you can also sprinkle them with fresh lemon juice.

Serve warm with chicory coffee or another strong blend.

SERVES 8 TO 10

Note: Orange granules are available on the Internet from www.oregonspice.com.

JACOB'S NAN

SERVE THESE INDIAN FRIED BREADS WITH CURRIES AND TANDOORI DISHES.

½ cup milk

½ cup yogurt

½ teaspoon baking soda

1 teaspoon sugar

4 tablespoons butter or
     margarine, melted

2 eggs, lightly beaten

3 (¼-ounce) packets dry yeast

3 cups flour

½ teaspoon salt

Oil for frying

In a medium pan over medium-low heat, warm the milk and stir in the yogurt until thoroughly mixed. Remove the pan from the heat. Add the baking soda, sugar, 2 tablespoons butter, the eggs, and dry yeast. Set aside.

In a large bowl, sift together the flour and the salt. Make a well in the flour and gradually add the warmed milk-yogurt mixture, stirring it into the flour as you pour.

Knead the flour for 10 to 15 minutes until it becomes smooth and elastic. Brush the dough with some of the remaining 2 tablespoons butter. Cover the dough with a warm, damp cloth and set the nan aside in a warm place for 1 to 1½ hours, or until the dough has risen to twice its size.

Preheat the oven broiler to high.

Heat the oil in a deep fryer to 375 degrees F.

Knead the dough again for a few minutes, having first floured both hands, and divide the dough into 8 equal-sized pieces. On a floured surface use a heavy rolling pin to roll each piece into an 8- to 10-inch pancake. Cover the pancakes with a warm, damp cloth for another 20 minutes.

Slide nans, one at a time, into the hot oil and cook them until they start to brown and float on the surface, 30 seconds to 1 minute.

Remove cooked nans and drain them on paper towels. Brush one side of each nan with the remaining butter and the other side with warm water. Place the warm-water side of the nans under your oven broiler for about 2 minutes.

SERVES 8

MR. DOBB'S COWBOY BREAD

½ cup boiling water

¾ cup cold milk

1 teaspoon sugar

1½ teaspoons dry yeast
   (about ½ packet)

1 egg, beaten

2 tablespoons butter, melted
   and cooled

¼ teaspoon salt

¼ teaspoon ground nutmeg

4 cups flour

Oil for frying

In a large bowl, stir together the water, milk, and sugar. Sprinkle the yeast over the top, and let the mixture stand for 5 minutes to dissolve the yeast.

Stir the egg and butter into the yeast mixture, then stir in the salt, nutmeg, and 2 cups of the flour. Mix until everything is well blended. Mix in the remaining flour, ½ cup at a time, until the dough pulls away from the side of the bowl. Turn the dough out onto a floured surface, and knead for 10 *full* minutes.

Place the dough into a greased bowl, in a warm spot in the kitchen, and let it rise until doubled in size, about 30 minutes.

Heat oil in a deep fryer to 350 degrees F.

Divide the dough into 8 balls, and let them rest for another 20 minutes. Roll each ball flat to 8 to 10 inches in diameter.

Using a slotted spoon or spatula, gently slip each of the pieces of bread into the hot oil and cook for 30 to 60 seconds on each side, or until light to medium brown spots appear.

Remove the bread from the heat with a spoon or spatula and keep it covered with a damp cloth, or store in a Ziploc plastic bag, until serving time. Serve warm with plenty of real butter and homemade preserves.

SERVES 4 TO 8

NARGISI PURI

2 eggs, boiled, peeled, and finely chopped

2 medium potatoes, boiled, peeled, and mashed

1 tablespoon chopped fresh mint

1 green chili, seeded and finely chopped

2 teaspoons salt

1½ cups flour

2 tablespoons vegetable oil

2 tablespoons warm water

Oil for frying

Heat the oil in a deep fryer to 350 degrees F.

In a small bowl, knead together the eggs, potatoes, mint, chili, and 1 teaspoon salt and divide the mixture into 8 portions. In a separate bowl, sieve the flour and the remaining 1 teaspoon salt. Add to the potato mixture, then add the vegetable oil. Mix the ingredients well, approximately 5 minutes. Slowly add the warm water. Knead to a soft dough.

Divide the dough into 8 equal parts and shape them into balls. Roll each ball out to about 2 inches in diameter. Place one portion of egg mixture in the center of each ball. Fold it over and pinch the ends. Now roll out each into a round puri, 4 inches in diameter. Do not make them too thin or the stuffing will come out.

Deep-fry 1 or 2 at a time until the pastries turn golden, 2 to 3 minutes.

Serve hot with plain yogurt.

SERVES 6 TO 8

NAVAJO FRY BREAD

4 cups flour

1 tablespoon baking powder

1 teaspoon salt

1 teaspoon sugar

1½ cups water

½ cup honey for drizzling

Confectioners' sugar for
   sprinkling

Oil for frying

Heat the oil in a deep fryer to 350 degrees F.

In a medium bowl, mix the flour, baking powder, salt, and sugar. Add the water and mix well, until it reaches a doughlike consistency. Knead the dough on a floured board till it becomes elastic, then let it rest for 10 minutes, covered with a moist towel.

On a floured surface, roll out the dough till it is ½ inch thick. Cut it into 4-inch circles. Deep-fry them 1, or at most 2, at a time, till the bread is golden brown, 2 to 3 minutes, then drain the cooked fry breads on paper towels.

Drizzle with the honey, or sprinkle with the confectioners' sugar, and serve.

SERVES 6 TO 8

PARISIAN BREAKFAST BREAD

4 eggs

¾ cup light cream

¾ cup whole milk

¼ cup granulated sugar

1 teaspoon vanilla extract

1 teaspoon grated lemon zest

6 (¾-inch-thick) slices stale French, Italian, or challah bread

Confectioners' sugar for sprinkling

Ground cinnamon for sprinkling

Ground nutmeg for sprinkling

Oil for frying

In a large bowl, beat the eggs, cream, milk, sugar, vanilla, and lemon zest until well mixed and a frothy yellow color.

Place the bread slices in a flat baking dish and pour the egg mixture over the slices, turning them over carefully after 5 minutes to coat both sides. Refrigerate, covered, overnight.

Heat 2 inches of oil in a Dutch oven or deep pan to 375 degrees F. Preheat the oven to 200 degrees F.

Carefully slide each slice of bread into the hot oil using a large spatula. Fry the bread, 1 or 2 at a time, for 1½ minutes each side, lift from the oil with a slotted spoon or spatula, and drain on a paper towel. Keep the bread warm on a plate in the oven until all the slices are done.

Serve the bread warm. Sprinkle the bread with confectioners' sugar, cinnamon, and nutmeg.

SERVES 4 TO 6

PORTUGUESE FRIED BREAD

2 cups flour

3 teaspoons baking powder

½ teaspoon salt

¼ cup plus 2 tablespoons
    sugar

¾ cup milk

2 tablespoons ground
    cinnamon

Honey for drizzling

Oil for frying

Heat the oil in a deep fryer to 350 degrees F, or heat 1 to 2 inches of oil in a Dutch oven.

Whisk together the flour, baking powder, salt, and 2 tablespoons sugar. Add the milk, and knead until it reaches a doughlike, smooth consistency.

Divide the resulting dough into 16 to 20 balls. Pat them each out on a flat, floured surface to ½ inch thick.

Fry the dough pieces, 1 or 2 at a time, browning both sides for 3 to 4 minutes.

Remove from the oil with a slotted spoon or spatula, drain on paper towels, and serve warm.

In a small bowl, mix the cinnamon and remaining ¼ cup sugar to sprinkle over the warm breads. You may also drizzle honey over the cooked fry breads.

SERVES 8 TO 10

SANTA MARIA DEEP-FRIED BREAKFAST BISCUITS

IF YOU'RE IN A HURRY, YOU CAN USE FROZEN PREPACKAGED BISCUITS FROM THE GROCERY STORE. USE THE SMALL 2-INCH-DIAMETER BISCUITS BECAUSE THE "GRAND," OR LARGE, VARIETY DON'T COOK THROUGH.

1½ (¼-ounce) packets dry yeast

½ cup warm water (105 degrees F)

2 cups milk, room temperature

2 tablespoons sugar

½ cup shortening or lard

1 tablespoon salt

4½ cups flour

Oil for frying

In a small bowl, add the yeast to the warm water and let the mixture sit for 5 minutes. Add the milk, sugar, shortening or lard, salt, and flour, and mix well with a large spoon. Roll the dough 1 inch thick on a floured board and using a biscuit or cookie cutter, cut the dough into 2-inch circles. Set the dough aside and let the biscuits rise by about 50 percent, about 1 hour.

Heat the oil in a deep fryer to 350 degrees F.

Slip the biscuits into the hot oil, 3 to 4 at a time, and fry them until they puff up and are golden on both sides. Remove them from the hot oil with a slotted spoon and drain the biscuits on paper towels. Serve hot.

MAKES 36 TO 40 BISCUITS

SOPHIA'S SOPAIPILLAS

THESE ARE DELICIOUS DRIZZLED WITH HONEY OR STUFFED WITH REFRIED BEANS, CHILI, CHOPPED ONION, GRATED CHEESE, AND GUACAMOLE.

1¼ cups milk

4 cups flour, sifted

1½ teaspoons salt

1 teaspoon baking powder

1 tablespoon lard (or butter)

1 (¼-ounce) packet dry yeast

¼ cup warm water (115 degrees F)

Oil for frying

In a medium saucepan, scald the milk, then set the pan off the heat and let it cool to room temperature.

In a medium bowl, combine the flour, salt, and baking powder. Cut the lard or butter into the flour with a pastry cutter or fork. In another medium bowl, dissolve the yeast in the warm water. Add the cooled, scalded milk.

Make a well in the center of the flour mixture and add the milk mixture slowly, working it into the dough, until the dough is firm and springy and holds its shape, 2 to 3 minutes. Cover the dough with a damp towel or invert the bowl over the dough and set it aside at room temperature for about 10 minutes.

Heat the oil in a deep fryer to 350 degrees F.

Roll one fourth of the dough to a ¼-inch thickness, then cut it into 3-inch triangles; do not reroll any of the dough. Continue with the remaining dough, a quarter at a time, until all the dough is cut into triangles.

To assure puffing, slightly stretch each piece of dough before lowering it into the oil. Cover the cut dough with a towel as you fry the sopaipillas, a few at a time, in hot oil.

They should puff up and become hollow very soon after being slipped into the oil. Hold each piece of dough under the surface with tongs or a slotted spoon until the dough puffs, about 30 seconds. Remove the sopaipillas with a slotted spoon and drain on paper towels. Serve hot with any Southwestern meal.

SERVES 6 TO 8

VIRGIN ISLANDS JOHNNYCAKES

2 cups flour

2 tablespoons baking
   powder

1 teaspoon sugar

1 teaspoon salt

2 tablespoons shortening
   (Crisco works well)

⅓ cup warm water

Oil for frying

Combine the flour, baking powder, sugar, and salt in a mixing bowl. Add the shortening. Stir until the mixture resembles coarse crumbs. Add the water. Stir until a stiff but smooth dough forms. Knead the dough thoroughly, but lightly, until any lumps are gone. Place the dough on a floured board, cover it with a damp towel, and let it rest for 30 minutes.

Heat the oil in a deep fryer or Dutch oven to 350 degrees F.

Roll 2-inch pieces of dough into balls and flatten them. Fry both sides until golden, 3 to 4 minutes. Remove them from the oil with a slotted spoon or spatula, drain them on paper towels, and serve hot.

SERVES 6

DRIZZLED DROPCAKES

2 eggs, separated

¼ cup brown sugar

1 cup cake flour, sifted

1½ teaspoons baking powder

½ teaspoon cinnamon

¼ teaspoon salt

½ cup whole milk

Powdered sugar for
sprinkling

Oil for frying

Preheat the oil in a deep fryer to 365 degrees F.

In a medium mixing bowl, beat the egg yolks and sugar with a whisk or hand mixer until smooth and completely incorporated. In a separate bowl, combine the flour, baking powder, cinnamon, and salt. Add the flour mixture to the egg yolk mixture and stir, then add the whole milk and stir again until relatively smooth. In a separate bowl, using a hand mixer whip the egg whites until they form sharp peaks, then gently fold them into the batter.

Using a small ice cream scoop or a teaspoon, drop the batter into the hot oil and fry until golden brown, about 2 minutes, turning once.

Remove the cakes from the oil and drain them on paper towels. Sprinkle the warm cakes generously with powdered sugar and serve immediately.

SERVES 4 TO 6

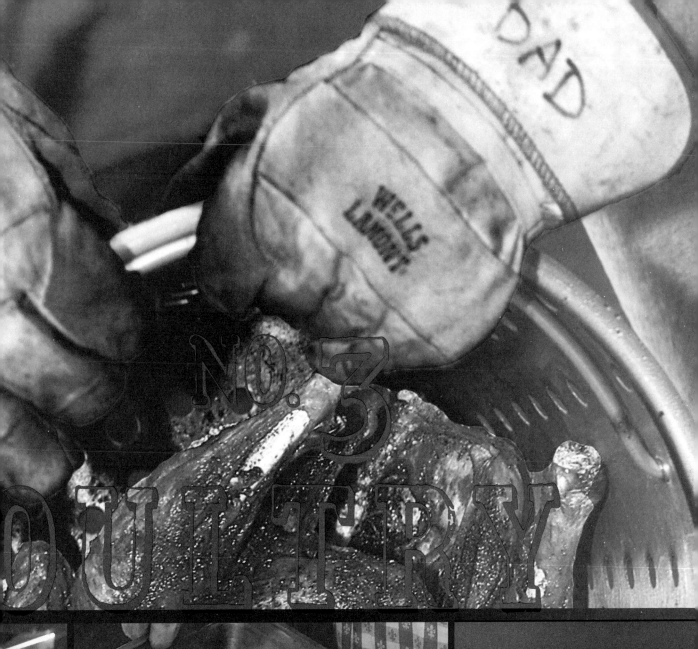

NO. 3
POULTRY

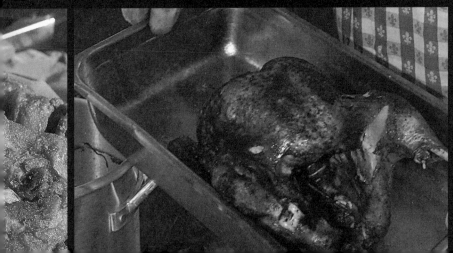

NO. 3

POULTRY

A DUMB BIRD IS HE

The domesticated turkey is probably the dumbest animal on the planet, next to perhaps gooney birds, paper clips, and lawn mold. But it's not their fault. It's because they've been bred, re-bred, and breaded some more, generation after generation, in captivity. Darwin's Laws of Natural Selection and Variation don't work when some bozo wearing horn-rimmed glasses and thongs feeds you, raises you, protects you, houses you, nurtures you, and then kills you. To be kind, one can say that turkeys lack "street savvy," or in this case even "turkey-pen savvy."

But over and above that, they're fat, weak, and probably couldn't fend for themselves if they were allowed to fend. They're clumsy, they're slower than a three-legged turtle, and, in a bid to prevent escapes from that turkey pen, each and every last one of 'em has been bred to not be able to fly. Sad to say they ain't much but good eatin'.

Two hundred seventy-six million turkeys were raised in the United States in 2001.

Continuing our dissing of the birds, turkeys are insecure, panic easily, and get "all het up" at the slightest change in their environment. Watch what happens in a flock of turkeys if you make a loud noise—instant bedlam, almost like a 75-percent (no a 90-percent) discount sale in lady's shoes at the Nordstrom Rack.

If there were turkey psychologists they'd make a fortune. When frightened, gazillions of frantic and frenetic birds run around in circles and flee smack dab into the nearest corner, wooden fence, or barn. And then dozens more birds behind *them* charge full speed into the same corner, fence, or barn and everyone ends up in a big pile of broken turkeys, the maimed and crippled ones on top smothering those even unluckier birds at the bottom.

Turkeys were first domesticated on our shores by Southwest Indians 2,000 years ago.

And guess what else? Turkeys have heart attacks. The United States Air Force was doing test runs and breaking the sound barrier near a turkey farm, where hundreds of turkeys dropped dead from heart attacks.

Urban legend aside, there are somewhat reliable, if you believe the old "I know people who know people who saw them" kinda stories, of young birds opening their thirsty mouths to raindrops pouring from the sky, but forgetting to close them and drowning in the one last quench of thirst. But we don't believe those stories . . . naaaa!

Wild turkeys can fly for short distances up to 55 miles per hour.

By the way, the bird's name is another mistake. A long time ago some folks thought the funny-looking birds came from—you guessed it—Turkey, when really they'd been here for years. But some dolt somehow got the idea that turkeys were guinea fowl that came from Islamic "Turkish" lands, and passed that on to someone else.

A few experts think the first Thanksgiving dinner was served by the Pilgrims sometime between September 21 and November 9, 1621. Or was it on July 30, 1623? Or was it November 29, 1621? You get the idea, no one really knows. Others credit the settlers of Virginia's Jamestown with celebrating the first Thanksgiving as their version of England's ancient Harvest Home Festival, since there were no bowl games to watch. I don't think there were, anyway.

For their first meal on the moon, astronauts Neil Armstrong and Edwin Aldrin ate roast turkey in foil packets.

And still another group of historians, who happened to be sitting in Newt's Olde Tyme Taverne swigging Rolling Rock last Sunday, swear that a guy named Morris Butterball started it all when he invited a few Pilgrim friends over for beer and some sorta bird. Oh yeah, Pilgrims didn't drink beer. In that case, he probably gave 'em some more lime Jell-O mold and an extra drumstick.

President Abraham Lincoln, much before he went to the theater, proclaimed Thanksgiving a national holiday in 1863, supposedly as a response to a campaign organized by a feisty magazine editor, Sarah Josepha Hale.

Henry VIII was the first English king to like eating turkey.

From 1846 to 1863, Ms. Hale, the editor of *Godey's Lady Book*, a sort of *Ladies' Home Journal* of the 1800s, and the author of "Mary Had a Little Lamb," embarked on a campaign to turn Thanksgiving into a national holiday during which workers would not be required to go to work. Yeah, Sarah! Her campaign resulted in Lincoln's Thanksgiving proclamation—the first such proclamation of a national Thanksgiving holiday since 1789, when George W. (the first George W. to become president—now there have been three) initially proclaimed a National Day of Thanksgiving, a holiday that was dropped by subsequent presidents.

But after Lincoln's rescue of the day, Thanksgiving has been celebrated as a national holiday, an American celebration of football and John Madden's six-legged turkeys, and a day in late November when we don't have to work. Thanks again, Sarah and Abe.

In 1939, President Franklin Roosevelt moved Thanksgiving from the last Thursday to the third Thursday in November. He wanted to help businesses (malls, discount stores, and Internet websites of the time) by lengthening the shopping period before Christmas. Today that shopping period seems to have grown to run from July 5 until Christmas. In 1941, this unpopular move (Teddy's Turkeygate?) inspired Congress to permanently fix the date on the fourth Thursday of November.

Tom Turkey's real name: Meleagris gallopavo!

Through the years this date has been circled on turkey calendars all over the world, and those few turkeys fortunate enough to see the following day's sunrise count themselves as really, really lucky. There are very few really, really lucky turkeys. It's a good thing that there has been

a good supply of them, otherwise we'd have used them all up by about 1953. August, I think.

In the year 2000, about 267 million turkeys were raised and it's estimated that 45 million of those turkeys were eaten at Thanksgiving, 22 million at Christmas, and 19 million at Easter. That leaves a whopping 181 million birds that someone musta cooked, and I'll betcha a lot of them were cooked below the Mason-Dixon Line.

> *In the early West, turkeys were trailed like cattle in "drives" to supply food where needed. One of the earliest turkey drives was over the Sierras from California to Carson City, Nevada. Hungry miners coughed up $5 apiece for the birds.*

By the way, in case you haven't noticed, we all owe a heap of gratitude to those Southerners for discovering many of the foods that make up the best, tastiest part of American's only indigenous cooking style: *barbecue.*

Back on the cotton-gin plantations it seems white folks didn't want pig ribs and skin and shoulders, preferring hams, bacon, and tenderloins. So they let the slaves have the rest. Bad move—for the plantation owners, anyway.

Result: Today's multibillion-dollar industry is selling those same pig ribs, pork shoulders, and cracklings to a whole passel of folks, including a few plantation owners. Where would barbecue be today if those plantation honchos had liked ribs? But let's go back to the subject of our conversation, turkey. *No, not you,* we were talking about the bird.

> *Big Bird, Sesame Street's oversized bird-of-some-sort, wears a costume made of turkey feathers.*

For years this noble fowl has been roasted, broiled, smoked, diced, sliced, quartered, fricasseed, baked, braised, grilled, barbecued, and cooked in any one of a number of other ways. But leave it to those clever Southern folks again to discover the "Number One, Top Drawer, Most Flavorful, Most Delicious" way ever invented to cook 'em.

Deep-fat-frying. The very thing our mothers, and now our wives, warn us against every day. Yup, taking a whole 12- to 22-pound bird and ceremoniously dunking him in 4½ to 5 gallons of boiling oil, and in the time it normally takes you to get the oven up to temperature, he's done. And there you are pulling out the most golden, most moist, best tastin' turkey you've ever wrapped your teeth around.

> *Turkeys are high in protein, low in fat, and low in cholesterol.*

We can't determine who first decided to deep-fry whole turkeys, but we admire their intuition, and let's call it what it is: "turkey-pen savvy." For this simple process has exploded on the American culinary scene today with more than 1,000,000 deep-frying units sold last year alone! Fer gosh sakes, even Emeril, Rosie, Regis, and, oh, yes, even Martha, are frying 'em on-screen. Hey, folks, that's a lotta oil, gas, birds, and greens. The kind of greens with presidential faces on the front, that is.

The biggest turkey on record was Tom Turkey Tyson, who weighed in at a hefty 85 pounds and was sold for £4,400 pounds in 1989. In today's dollars that's more than $6,500 American greenbacks. Try fittin' him in your oven.

Deep-frying turkeys, which started as a Southern tradition, has in just the past three years boiled its way across the nation in a veritable frenzy. If *you* haven't fried a turkey, odds are you've tasted one someone else fried up, saw someone show Martha Stewart how to do it, or read in some foodie magazine about the rapturous joys of deep-fried gobblers.

Purists say the deep-frying process seals the outside while the interior remains very juicy and the skin develops a crisp texture. Aficionados just say it tastes real gooooood.

A 16-week-old turkey is called a fryer. A 5- to 7-month-old turkey is called a young roaster, and a yearling is a year old. Any turkey 15 months or older is called mature. A 17-month-old turkey is called "Lucky."

Commercial caterers offer deep-fried turkey and restaurants feature the golden crisp bird during the holidays. At football stadium and baseball park tailgate parties, outdoor church suppers (do they still have these?), and neighborhood get-togethers, folks are setting up pots big enough to cook Volkswagens on their driveways, filling those pots with millions of gallons of precious oils, and lowering deceased birds into the stainless steel faster than a witch-dunking party in Salem, Massachusetts.

Since most of us buy our turkey birds frozen, there are three, and only three, safe ways to defrost turkeys:

- in the refrigerator
- in cold water
- in the microwave

Never defrost a turkey on the kitchen counter, in front of a Duraflame log in your fireplace, or wrapped in foil and strapped to the engine of a '56 Ford truck. And please don't be like a certain Darwin Award loser who tried to defrost a 24-pound bird in the dishwasher, then cooked it the next day. The salmonella he contracted fried *him*.

In 2000, the average American ate 17.75 pounds of turkey.

To completely thaw a frozen 20-pound turkey the safest, most reliable, and slowest way, you'll need about five days in your nearest refrigerator.

Or if you want to speed things a tad, put "Tom," plastic wrapping and all, in a kitchen sink of *cold* water in his see-through polystyrene suit, submerging him completely and changing the water every 30 minutes to be sure it stays cold. Depending on the size of the fowl he/she could be thawed in as little as 2 to 3 hours, or as long as 5 to 6 hourss.

Turkeys have been around the planet for a mere 10 million years.

While some people say that turkey defrosted in a microwave is okay, many more say it's another open ticket to an intimate visit from either of the twins: *Salmonella* serotype *Typhimurium* or *Salmonella* serotype *Enteritidis*. You'll be inviting guests to a sort of a modern day "last supper." *Your* last supper!

If thawed by this method you should cook Mr. Turkey like *right now*, because some hidden parts of him may well have become warm and provide a spalike refuge for those salmonella twins during microwaving. Waiting to cook your bird for a few hours after microwave defrosting is like playing Russian roulette with maybe only three bullets in a six-chamber gun. Spin, click. Spin, click. Spin, *blllaaam!*

Male turkeys (Toms) gobble, females (hens) click when they speak.

The United States Department of Agriculture says that this is the right way to cook Tommy Turkey: "For whole turkeys the USDA recommends 180°F for thigh meat, 170°F for breast meat, and 165°F for stuffing, whether cooked alone or in the bird." Said temperature is to be taken before or immediately after removing the turkey from the oven. But their own material also says anything more than 160°F is safe. Here is a highly technical graphic to indicate turkey "safe" temperatures. Please don't tell them I've got this.

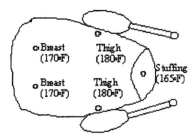

I personally cook turkey to a thigh temperature of 170 to 175 degrees F. The breast meat will be a bit moister, you're perfectly safe according to *every* health source we contacted, and there are no known bacteria that can stand that high a temperature.

Just about everyone says that the bird isn't the problem, but the stuffing can be a *big* problem. In fact, improperly cooked stuffing is thought to be the cause of most turkey food poisoning. But since deep-fried turkeys are *never* stuffed, we're gonna happily go our own way and bring him out from the heat or hot oil when he's reached the safe 170-degree temperature, letting him rest, covered in foil, for 15 to 20 minutes so his internal juices retract back into the meat. Then we're gonna carve him up and eat 'im.

Ben Franklin thought the eagle of "bad moral character" and actively sought to make the turkey our national bird.

So we hope we jawed on long enough to make you hungry. In the words of my aunt Rhoda: "Let's go out to git ourselves a dad gurn turkey bird to fry up!"

DEEP-FRYING A WHOLE TURKEY: TIPS, TECHNIQUES, AND SAFETY GUIDELINES

Compiled from safety and cooking guidelines from the FDA, the National Turkey Federation, the Washington State Farm Bureau & Department of Health, Foster Farms, Butterball Inc., and Cabela's on-line website.

First, before you do anything, follow the manufacturer's directions and check for gas leaks when you hook your burner up to a propane or natural gas line. *Every time you turn it on,* you should perform a simple test by putting soapy water on all joints to see if any gas leaks through the soap bubbles.

Where to cook? Do not set up your deep fryer on your lawn, unless you want to get rid of the section of lawn it'll be standing on. Unless you're a genius and don't spill any oil it'll kill your lawn quickern' a gallon of Roundup. And it will probably attract insects and nocturnal critters investigating that nice "oily-fatty" smell you've left there.

Best find a gravel driveway, or section of garden where the dirt is nice and flat. If you have to set up on a cement driveway at least put down a large piece of cardboard to sop up any spilled grease. Do not set up the deep fryer on your wooden deck. Let's see: boiling oil + propane gas flames + a wood surface. Nope.

Never, ever fry indoors. And that means inside a garage as well. There have been quite a few houses that fried up along with the turkey in boiling oil when it caught on fire. Plus the smell of frying foods will linger for days, and you'd probably not want to have that scent hanging inside your garage or, most certainly, your kitchen.

Have an ABC fire extinguisher ready at hand. *Do not use water to put out any oil fire.* Water and oil do not mix so you could actually make the problem worse by spreading the oil all over the place with water, plus hot oil virtually explodes when it's contacted by water. Use the pot lid or a large sheet of aluminum foil to smother flames, and if that isn't possible, hit it with the extinguisher.

Have large pot holders or, better yet, fireproof barbecuing gloves handy, too. Wear gloves, a long-sleeved shirt, long pants, and covered shoes. Errant drops of 350-degree grease can wreak havoc on exposed skin. Safety glasses or sunglasses aren't a bad idea as well.

Measure your oil properly, using How Much Oil Do I Need? (page 4). Don't guess. Fill the pot with oil to that level only. Place the pot on the burner and light a fire to start the oil cooking. Use an appropriate deep-fry thermometer with a very long probe to measure the temperature in the center of the oil. Bringing room temperature oil to 350 to 375 degrees F can take anywhere from 45 minutes to 1 hour.

Prepare the turkey at this time: injecting it, rubbing it inside and outside, marinating it, whatever. But do not—I repeat, *do not*—stuff the turkey. Deep-fry empty turkeys only. If you want stuffing, mix it up, put it in foil or in a covered pot, and cook it in the kitchen oven.

If your turkey has one of those cute lil' pop-up temperature thingees, completely remove it, and, if you marinate the turkey, remember to pat it dry inside and out before you cook it. Liquid on the surface can cause face- or arm-scarring burns as the hot oil reacts to the liquid.

Do not heat oil beyond the recommended temperature for the kind of oil you're using. If the oil begins to smoke it's too hot and may suddenly flame up. Then you have 4 to 5 gallons of boiling *and* flaming oil. Not a good way to start your day.

Once the cooking oil has reached the right temperature you're ready to fry up the bird. But again a few safety precautions are called for, unless, that is, you wish to get a costly, painful, and lengthy tour of your local hospital's burn ward.

Make sure the turkey is dry (inside and out), at room temperature (or nearly so), and carefully place it in a turkey basket, or on a lifting rod or hook. In a cooking basket it doesn't matter which end is up, but on most lifting hooks the "arse end," or tail end, of the turkey should be down. Make sure it's secure and won't fall off, splashing hot oil on you, when you try to lower it into the pot.

Before lowering the bird into the hot oil, *turn off* the gas under the pot. You do not want to spill oil onto a lit flame. Trust me on this. Carefully and slowly lower the turkey into the hot oil, lifting up and down several times as you lower it into the oil so that the liquid can begin filling the inner cavities of the turkey. Don't rush it. Clip a deep-frying or candy thermometer to the edge of the pot so you can check the temperature anytime during cooking.

When the turkey is completely under the oil, *turn the gas flame back on* and begin your timer. The oil temperature may also have fallen, so adjust the flame to go back up to 350 degrees F and then adjust the flame again to keep the oil at that temperature for the rest of the cooking time.

Whole turkeys require 3 to 4 minutes per pound. That's right, 3 to 4 *minutes*. So a 20-pound turkey should be done in approximately 1 hour! That's a lot better than the standard 20 minutes per pound in a conventional oven. And we haven't even talked about the taste difference.

Immediately wash *everything* that has touched, or been touched by, the raw turkey—including your hands, all implements, injectors, spoons, knives, countertops, and cutting boards—with hot soap and water. Rinse and dry. Saran, the folks who brought us Rap (er, Wrap), have just come out with Cutting Sheets, a disposable plastic and paper sheet that you place on a counter or cutting board to handle turkeys, chickens or other food. It keeps juices and fluids from touching the surface you're working on and, after you're finished, you just throw it away.

While the turkey is merrily bubbling away in his hot oil bath you must *never leave the burner unattended*. A pet, a neighbor's child, or one of your own, may come by and investigate the fun thing you're doing in the backyard.

When the time has come to check the turkey you must again *turn off the gas* before removing the bird from the hot oil.

If you can, have someone slowly and carefully lift the bird partially out of the oil so you can check the thigh and breast temperatures. If you're by yourself, set the turkey in a large pan on the table or counter while you take a meat thermometer and check the temperature at four different spots on Mr. Turkey.

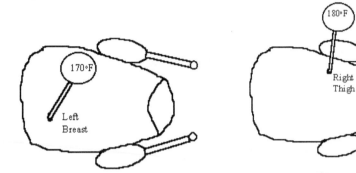

First check *both* sides of the breast to make sure the temperature is 170 degrees F. Then check *both* thighs to see if they are at 180 degrees F. If so, the bird passes and is on the way to dinner.

If any of the temperatures are below those levels you must put the turkey back in the oil (following the same safety procedures as when you began to cook it) and cook until those temperatures are reached. Those are the safe guidelines laid down by the USDA and strictly followed by most other government health agencies, state and local health departments, turkey producers, restaurants, and deep-fry equipment manufacturers.

But since our turkey passed the temperature test we'll finish up here. Set the bird upright in a large bowl, pot, or pan, so the oil inside can drain out, and cover the entire bird loosely with aluminum foil. Let it rest for 10 to 15 minutes so that the juices flow back from the outside toward the center of the bird, while the oil flows into the container the bird is sittin' in.

Meanwhile, cover the oil and let it cool until it's reached the ambient temperature. Carefully using a filter pump, drain the oil back into its original container or into a large dark glass or plastic bottle. If you don't have a pump, carefully pour the oil in small batches through filtration into the same containers. Place used oil in a cool, dark spot until next time. You may wish to use a marker and mark the date on the bottle of oil so you can keep track of how long the oil has been in use.

Carve and serve the turkey as usual. If you wish to avoid some of the cholesterol in the bird, remove the skin before you serve the meat. The bulk of any cholesterol in turkey, and in all poultry, is in the skin, not the meat.

When the meal is finished (fantastic, wasn't it?), cover and refrigerate any leftover meat. Freeze what you can't eat in 2 to 3 days.

TURKEY DEEP-FRYING CHECKLIST

Heavy-duty portable propane burner

Propane tank

ABC fire extinguisher

26- to 40-quart stockpot

Turkey holder (e.g., stand, cradle, vertical rack, or metal drain basket)

Lowering mechanism (e.g., broom handle)

Turkey

Marinade

Hypodermic meat injector

Dry rub

Peanut oil, 2 to 5 gallons for deep-frying pot

Heavy oven mitts, leather gloves, or fireproof barbecue gloves

Long-sleeved shirt, long pants, closed shoes

Safety or sunglasses (optional)

Large platter

Deep-frying thermometer (or candy thermometer)

Aluminum foil

Meat thermometer

Paper towels

Soap and water

An assistant

A comfortable chair

A chilled adult beverage

A good book

AH, THERE'S THE RUB!

Turkey, chicken, duck, and game hen rubs

THE INGREDIENTS IN THE FOLLOWING RUBS SHOULD BE MIXED TOGETHER WELL, RUBBED GENTLY INTO THE FRESH POULTRY, AND LEFT TO DRY-MARINATE FOR AT LEAST 4 HOURS, BUT PREFERABLY OVERNIGHT. IF YOU HAVE LEFTOVER RUB, DISCARD IT, BUT THESE AMOUNTS WILL COVER A 20- TO 24-POUND BIRD WITH AN ADEQUATE DUSTING.

WHITE KNIGHT RUB

¼ cup onion powder

¼ cup ground white pepper

1 tablespoon salt

2 tablespoons garlic powder

2 tablespoons sugar

ROMANOV RUB

1 clove garlic, crushed

10 allspice berries, crushed

½ teaspoon finely chopped rosemary leaves

2 tablespoons olive oil

CURRIED RUB

¼ cup chili powder

1 teaspoon onion powder

1 teaspoon curry powder

1 teaspoon ground cumin

1 teaspoon garlic powder

1 teaspoon dry mustard

1 teaspoon white pepper

1 teaspoon dried oregano

2 teaspoons celery salt

1 teaspoon parsley flakes

BOBTAIL RUB

- 3 tablespoons mild paprika
- 2 teaspoons seasoned salt
- 2 teaspoons freshly ground black pepper
- 2 teaspoons garlic powder
- 1 teaspoon cayenne pepper, not too hot
- 1 teaspoon summer savory
- 1 teaspoon dry mustard
- ½ teaspoon chili powder
- 1 teaspoon ground thyme
- 1 teaspoon ground coriander
- 2 teaspoons green peppercorns
- 1 teaspoon ground allspice

BRANDY'S RUBBING POWDER

- 1 teaspoon garlic powder
- 1 tablespoon honey granules
- ½ teaspoon ground thyme
- 1 tablespoon lemon granules
- 1 tablespoon Worcestershire powder
- 1 teaspoon sugar

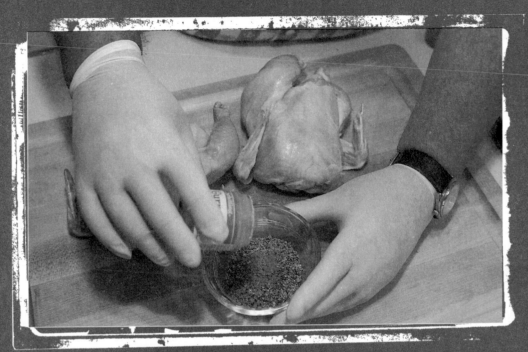

CASABLANCA RUB

2 tablespoons paprika

1 teaspoon salt

1 teaspoon sugar

½ teaspoon coarsely ground black pepper

½ teaspoon ground ginger

½ teaspoon ground cardamom

½ teaspoon ground cumin

½ teaspoon ground fenugreek

½ teaspoon ground cloves

¼ teaspoon ground cinnamon

¼ teaspoon ground allspice

¼ teaspoon cayenne pepper

RED RIVER RUB

1 teaspoon cayenne pepper

1 teaspoon curry powder

1 teaspoon turmeric

1 teaspoon ground ginger

1 teaspoon ground cumin

1 tablespoon chili powder

1 tablespoon paprika

Dash of nutmeg

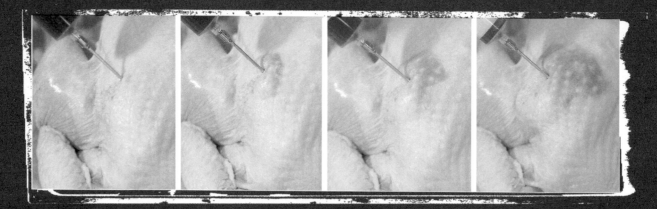

STICKIN' IT TO THE TURKEY
231 MARINADES FOR YOU

Place the uncooked turkey in a pan. Load your favorite marinade into a hypodermic meat injector (like the Cajun injector). Inject the marinade in multiple places on the turkey, especially through the breast, thighs, thick part of the wings, and legs. Marinate for 12 to 36 hours in the refrigerator.

There are about a zillion and three commercially bottled marinades available on the Internet, in grocery stores, in supermarkets, and in barbeque stores. Or, if you're cheap like me and like to mess around in the kitchen anyway, go to the following website and look over a list of 231 marinades you can do yourself: http://www.recipesource.com/side-dishes/marinades/indexall.html.

Put ingredients for each of the following marinades in a saucepan and heat until well mixed. Cool and inject into turkeys, chicken, game hens, or IRS agents. Each recipe is enough for a 12- to 15-pound bird.

ALLIGATOR MARINADE

- 4 ounces liquid garlic*
- 4 ounces liquid onion*
- 4 ounces liquid celery*
- 1 tablespoon ground red pepper
- 2 tablespoons salt
- 2 tablespoons Louisiana hot sauce
- 1 ounce liquid crab boil* OR 1 tablespoon Old Bay Seasoning

*Available at gourmet or specialty food stores.

LEMON BARBECUE MARINADE

- ½ cup lemon juice
- ¼ cup vegetable oil
- ½ teaspoon salt
- 1 teaspoon garlic powder
- 1 teaspoon onion powder
- ½ teaspoon ground black pepper
- ½ teaspoon ground thyme
- 1 teaspoon Worcestershire sauce

MAMA MIA'S MARINADE

- ⅔ cup Wishbone Italian dressing
- ⅓ cup sherry (regular, not the cooking kind)
- 2 teaspoons garlic powder
- 1 tablespoon lemon pepper
- 1 teaspoon onion powder
- 2 teaspoons cayenne pepper

TAHITI MARINADE

⅓ cup vinegar

¼ cup soy sauce

⅓ cup water

¼ cup fresh lime juice

¼ teaspoon garlic powder

⅛ teaspoon ground black pepper

PINEAPPLE MARINADE

¼ cup soy sauce

½ cup pineapple juice

¼ cup rice wine vinegar

¼ cup packed brown sugar

¾ teaspoon garlic powder

MINUTE MARINADE

1 cup Italian vinaigrette

1 cup white wine

Juice of 1 lemon

¼ cup butter, melted

POPEYE MARINADE

2 tablespoons kosher salt

2 teaspoons garlic powder

2 teaspoons white pepper

1 teaspoon cayenne pepper

½ teaspoon onion powder

1 cup butter, melted

WILD TURKEY MARINADE

⅓ cup red wine vinegar

⅓ cup olive oil

⅓ cup Wild Turkey whiskey

2 tablespoons garlic powder

5 teaspoons lemon pepper

5 teaspoons onion powder

2 to 3 teaspoons cayenne pepper

2 teaspoons paprika

1 teaspoon cumin

2 teaspoons black pepper

1 teaspoon sugar

1 teaspoon dried oregano

CAJUN DEEP-FRIED TURKEY

IT IS IMPORTANT TO STRAIN THE ITALIAN DRESSING SO THERE ARE NO SOLID PIECES.

MARINADE

1 cup Italian dressing, strained

¼ cup Louisiana hot sauce

2 tablespoons liquid smoke

¼ cup garlic powder

2 tablespoons seasoned salt

1 (10- to 12-pound) turkey, defrosted

1 cup Cajun seasoning, or favorite rub mix

Oil for frying

Mix the marinade ingredients together and add enough water to make 1 quart of marinade.

Remove the giblets from the turkey, then wash and pat it dry, especially inside the cavity. Using a food syringe, inject the marinade equally in each side of the breast and in each thigh and leg. Rub inside the cavity and all of the outside of the bird with the Cajun seasoning or rub mix. Marinate the turkey in the refrigerator for at least 24 hours, but if you can, marinate for 2 to 3 days.

When you're ready to cook the turkey, heat the oil in a deep fryer to 360 degrees F, using a deep-frying thermometer to check the temperature.

Place the bird on a turkey basket or holder. *Shut off the gas flame.* Slowly lower the basket into the oil, stopping, turning, and lifting it slightly as needed to prevent splattering, until the bird is submerged. *Turn the gas back on and relight.*

Cook 3 to 4 minutes per pound (30 to 40 minutes), or until the temperature in the thigh is 180 degrees and the breast is 170 degrees F.

When finished, *turn the gas off.* Then slowly lift the turkey out of the pot and drain it on paper towels, covered with foil, for about 20 minutes.

Carve the turkey and enjoy.

SERVES 8 TO 10

CURRIED TURKEY BREAST

RUB

1 tablespoon salt

1 tablespoon paprika

1 tablespoon brown sugar

1 tablespoon poultry
  seasoning

1 tablespoon ground black
  pepper

1 tablespoon ground cumin

2 tablespoons mild curry
  powder

1 tablespoon dried thyme

1 (3- to 5-pound) turkey
  breast

Oil for frying

In a small bowl, mix all of the rub ingredients and stir to blend completely. Gently massage the rub mixture into the turkey breast, covering all surfaces. Let it rest at room temperature for 1 hour.

Heat the oil in a deep fryer or Dutch oven to 350 degrees F.

Turn off the gas to avoid spilling oil on the flame. Place the turkey in a deep-fryer basket or use tongs and *slowly* lower the bird into the oil.

Turn on the gas. The breast should cook for 7 minutes per pound of meat and add 5 minutes to get a total cooking time (3 pounds of turkey breast $\times$ 7 minutes per pound = 21 minutes + 5 additional minutes = 26 minutes total cooking time).

When the cooking time is complete turn the gas *off* and remove the breast slowly to avoid spilling the oil. Use tongs or a turkey lifter to remove the bird if you cooked it in a Dutch oven. Drain on paper towels and let the breast sit for 10 minutes covered in foil.

Cool and serve.

SERVES 6 TO 8

BEER-BATTERED CHICKEN

SERVE THESE STRIPS WITH HONEY MUSTARD BEER DIP, WHICH YOU MAKE BY MIXING ¼ CUP HONEY MUSTARD AND ¼ CUP BEER UNTIL SMOOTH.

1½ pounds boneless, skinless chicken breast halves

1½ cups flour

1 teaspoon baking powder

2 eggs, beaten

½ cup beer

1 teaspoon salt

½ teaspoon cayenne pepper

1 tablespoon summer savory

Oil for frying

Rinse the chicken, and slice it into 1-inch strips.

In a medium bowl, stir together 1 cup flour and the baking powder. Mix in the beaten eggs and beer and set aside. Place the remaining ½ cup flour in a small brown paper bag, add the salt, cayenne pepper, and savory, and shake to mix well.

Heat the oil in a Dutch oven or deep fryer to 375 degrees F. Preheat the oven to 200 degrees F.

Drop the chicken strips into the bag and shake well to coat evenly. Dip the floured strips into the batter. Fry a few at a time in the hot oil, turning once, until the coating is golden brown on both sides, 4 to 5 minutes.

Remove the strips from the hot oil with tongs or a slotted spoon, drain on paper towels, and keep them warm on a platter in the oven until ready to serve.

SERVES 4 TO 6

BUTTERMILK FRIED CHICKEN

2 cups buttermilk

1½ teaspoons salt

½ teaspoon freshly ground
   black pepper

3 pounds frying chicken
   pieces

1 cup flour

Oil for frying

Combine the buttermilk with half the salt and pepper. Put the chicken in a Ziploc bag and pour the mixture over the chicken pieces, turn all the pieces to coat them well, and refrigerate them overnight.

Heat oil in a Dutch oven or deep fryer to 365 degrees F.

In a medium bowl, mix the flour and other half of the salt and pepper. Drain the marinade from the chicken pieces and using either a paper bag or shallow dish, coat the chicken pieces in the flour mixture, shake off the excess, and place the pieces in a single layer on a sheet of waxed paper.

Carefully add the chicken pieces to the hot oil and cook for 5 to 7 minutes, with the lid on. Remove the lid, turn the chicken, and cook the pieces for another 5 to 7 minutes with the lid on. Remove the lid and cook them for another 8 to 10 minutes until the skin is crispy.

Remove the chicken pieces with tongs and drain the pieces on paper towels.

Serve immediately on a heated platter.

SERVES 4 TO 6

CHICKEN IN A BLANKET

Parchment-wrapped chicken

4 scallions, green tops only

2 large boneless, skinless
chicken breasts

4 teaspoons minced
fresh ginger

2 teaspoons rice wine

2 teaspoons soy sauce

1 teaspoon salt

¼ teaspoon white pepper

1 teaspoon sugar

24 (6-inch) squares
parchment paper

2 teaspoons oil

1 cup teriyaki or hoisin
sauce, for dipping

Oil for frying

Shred the scallions lengthwise and then cut them into 1½-inch lengths. Cut the chicken breasts into strips ½-inch wide by 1½ inches in length.

Put the minced ginger in a garlic press and squeeze out 1 teaspoon of ginger juice. In a medium bowl, combine the ginger juice with the wine, scallions, soy sauce, salt, pepper, and sugar, to make a marinade for the chicken strips. Let the chicken marinate at room temperature in a covered container for at least 30 minutes.

Heat the oil in a deep fryer to 375 degrees F.

Place a square of parchment on your work surface, with one corner toward you. Rub a little oil in the center of the paper and place 1 piece of chicken and some scallion mixture on the paper horizontally, well below the center of the angled square.

Fold the lower corner up to cover the meat, then fold the left corner over to the right and the right corner over to the left, to make a small envelope. Fold the top corner down and tuck it in securely. Repeat using all the parchment paper squares and the rest of the chicken and scallions.

Deep-fry 2 or 3 envelopes at a time in the hot oil for 1 minute on each side. Remove them with a slotted spoon or a spatula, and drain them on paper towels.

Serve them with the teriyaki or hoisin sauce on the side for dipping. Each person gets 2 to 3 envelopes on his or her plate and everyone opens the envelopes as the meal begins.

SERVES 10 TO 12

COXHINA, COXHINA

Portuguese fried drumstick dumplings

3 boneless, skinless chicken
   breasts

½ medium onion, chopped

2 cloves garlic, finely
   chopped

2 cubes chicken bouillon

6 tablespoons butter

1½ teaspoons salt

½ teaspoon lemon pepper

4 cups water

¼ cup chopped fresh parsley

1 small green onion, chopped

3 cups flour

8 ounces cream cheese

2 egg whites

Bread crumbs

Oil for frying

In a large microwave-safe bowl, cook the chicken breasts, onion, garlic, chicken bouillon, butter, salt, lemon pepper, and water in a microwave oven on high. The chicken should be cooked through in 10 minutes.

Remove the chicken breasts and finely chop them. For color add the parsley and green onions.

In a medium saucepan, boil 3 cups of the remaining broth for 10 minutes to avoid salmonella poisoning. Add the flour and stir vigorously for about 1 minute until it becomes a moist dough. Take the dough out of the pan and cool it to a warm temperature. Knead it until it becomes smooth and all flour lumps are gone, about 10 minutes.

Heat oil in a deep fryer to 350 degrees F.

Flatten the dough to ¼-inch thickness with a rolling pin and cut 2½- to 3½-inch circles with a biscuit cutter or drinking glass. Place the dough in your palm, add 1 teaspoon of cream cheese and 1 teaspoon of the chicken filling. (Vary the amount of ingredients according to the size of the dough circle you cut so that you can close the dough with the filling staying inside.) Fold and close the dough in the shape of a drumstick (*coxhina* means a "little chicken drumstick" in Portuguese). Knead any unused scraps of dough and roll them again, cutting more circles until all the dough is used.

Brush the filled dough generously with egg whites and roll it in the bread crumbs until it is coated.

Deep-fry the coxhina for about 8 minutes or until golden brown. Remove from the hot oil with a slotted spoon or spatula. Drain on paper towels and serve hot.

SERVES 6 TO 8

DEEP-FRIED LEMON CORNISH HENS

2 (1½-pound) Cornish game hens
¼ cup fresh rosemary leaves
2 tablespoons lemon pepper
2 tablespoons dried lemon zest granules
1 teaspoon garlic powder
2 teaspoons salt
Lemon wedges for serving

Oil for frying

Rinse, clean, and wipe dry the game hens, patting them inside and out with a paper towel.

In a small bowl, mix the rosemary, lemon pepper, lemon zest granules, garlic, and salt. Reserve half of the mixture and set it aside. Rub the other half well into the hens, sprinkling them inside, too. Let them stand, covered, at room temperature for 1 hour.

Heat the oil in a deep fryer or Dutch oven to 375 degrees F. Carefully put the Cornish hens into the hot oil and deep-fry until golden brown, about 12 minutes.

To check for doneness, use a slotted spoon or tongs to carefully remove the hen from the pot and insert an instant-read thermometer in the thickest part of the thigh, not touching the bone—it should read 180 degrees. Drain on paper towels.

Transfer the hens to a wire rack and let them rest, covered, for 5 minutes. Serve them whole, or use a cleaver to split them in half lengthwise. Sprinkle each hen with the reserved spice/herb mixture and serve with lemon wedges.

SERVES 2 TO 4

GARLIC CHICKEN GOLF BALLS

2 pounds ground chicken (or pork)

½ teaspoon citrus pepper

½ teaspoon salt

½ teaspoon poultry seasoning

2 tablespoons soy sauce

2 tablespoons cornstarch

½ teaspoon freshly grated ginger

2 tablespoons marsala wine (or
    use a favorite sherry)

4 cloves garlic, minced

3 egg whites

COATING

1 cup cornstarch

1 cup flour

Oil for frying

Heat the oil in Dutch oven or deep fryer to 375 degrees F.

In a large bowl thoroughly mix the chicken or pork with the pepper, salt, poultry seasoning, soy sauce, cornstarch, ginger, wine, garlic, and egg whites. Let the mixture rest for 10 minutes, covered with plastic. With your hands form the chicken mixture into golf-ball-sized balls and set them on wax paper or aluminum foil.

To make the batter, mix the cornstarch with the flour and roll each ball in this mixture to coat evenly.

Slip the balls into the oil and cook until they float and are golden brown, about 5 minutes. Remove with a slotted spoon and drain on paper towels. Serve warm.

SERVES 8

GOLD NUGGETS

½ cup flour

1½ teaspoons garlic salt

1 teaspoon paprika

1 teaspoon ground sage

1 teaspoon onion powder

½ teaspoon white pepper

½ teaspoon poultry seasoning

½ cup water

1 egg, lightly beaten

3 whole boneless, skinless chicken
   breasts

1 bunch fresh parsley for garnish

Grated Parmesan cheese for garnish

Paprika for garnish

Oil for frying

Heat the oil in a deep fryer to 375 degrees F.

Combine the flour and seasonings in a medium glass bowl, add the water and egg, and stir well to make a smooth batter. Cut the chicken into 1½-inch-square nuggets.

Dip the chicken pieces into the batter, allowing any excess to drain. Slip 3 to 4 pieces at a time into the hot oil, and fry until crisp, 2 to 4 minutes. Drain the nuggets well on paper towels, then transfer the chicken to a warm platter garnished with fresh parsley. Sprinkle with grated Parmesan cheese and paprika and serve.

SERVES 6

KRISPY CREAMED QUAIL

THESE ARE SUPER SERVED WITH CRISP POTATO PANCAKES AND STIR-FRIED VEGGIES.

8 to 12 young farm-raised quail

2 cups coarsely chopped sweet onions

2 cups light cream

1 teaspoon Louisiana hot sauce

4 cups flour

2 tablespoons onion salt

1 teaspoon cayenne pepper

1 tablespoon brown sugar

2 teaspoons coarsely ground black pepper

Oil for frying

Wash the quail thoroughly under cold running water, making sure you remove any fat that may not have been removed during processing. Prick the quail all over with a sharp fork or small knife so the marinade can invade the insides and flavor the meat. Then set them in a 1- or 2-quart Ziploc sealable bag.

At this point sprinkle the chopped onions over the birds and immediately mix them in well so that the quail pick up the flavor of the onions. Close the bag and let them sit at room temperature for 30 minutes, rotating the bag often.

In a small bowl, blend together the cream and the hot sauce and pour it into the bag, over the quail and onions, to form a marinade. Let the birds marinate in the refrigerator overnight, or for at least 4 hours.

Just before you are ready to cook them, heat the oil to 350 degrees F in a deep fryer or deep Dutch oven.

Pour the flour into a large baking pan and add the salt, cayenne, sugar, and black pepper. Mix thoroughly.

Remove each quail from the marinade, and then liberally dust them in the coating mix, shake off the excess flour, and using tongs, carefully slip them into the hot oil.

Fry the quail for 10 to 12 minutes. The outside should be golden brown and crispy, and the inside should be light, moist, and delicately tender from the cream-onion marinade. Discard the marinade and the onions. Serve immediately.

SERVES 8 TO 12

LEMON CHICKEN STRIPS

2 pounds boneless, skinless chicken breasts

BATTER

½ **cup flour**

½ **cup cornstarch**

¼ **teaspoon garlic salt**

½ **teaspoon baking powder**

½ **teaspoon vegetable oil**

SAUCE

2 large lemons

3 tablespoons firmly packed brown sugar

½ **cup white wine**

1 teaspoon cornstarch

2 teaspoons water

Parsley sprigs for garnish

Oil for frying

Heat oil in Dutch oven or deep frying pot to 350 degrees F.

Cut the chicken into strips about 3 inches long by ½ inch wide. Place them in a shallow bowl, cover with plastic wrap, and set aside.

In a medium bowl, mix the batter ingredients, stirring until smooth.

Cut one lemon into ¼-inch slices and set aside. Squeeze the juice from the second lemon into a small bowl, add the sugar and white wine and stir well. Set aside.

In a small cup, mix the cornstarch and water. Stir to mix completely. Set aside.

Dip each piece of chicken into the batter and let the excess drip back into the bowl.

Deep-fry the chicken in small batches of 10 to 12 pieces. The chicken strips should brown up nicely in 4 to 5 minutes. Make sure they don't stick together.

Remove the finished strips from the oil with a slotted spoon and drain them on paper towels.

In a saucepan over high heat, bring the lemon-juice mixture to a boil for 4 to 5 minutes. Add the cornstarch mixture and stir it until the mixture is thickened.

Place the drained chicken pieces on a colorful plate, and garnish with lemon slices and parsley. Serve lemon sauce on the side.

SERVES 2 TO 4

PERTH DEEP-FRIED WINGS

16 chicken wings

½ cup soy sauce

7 tablespoons oyster sauce

½ cup sweet sherry

3 tablespoons lime juice

Salt and pepper to taste

1 cup flour

1 cup cornstarch

Oil for frying

Using a knife, poke holes in the wings, to allow the marinade to penetrate into the meat. Place the chicken wings in a glass dish, Ziploc bag, or stainless steel bowl.

In a small bowl, mix the soy sauce, oyster sauce, sherry, lime juice, salt, and pepper, and pour the mixture over the chicken. Cover the dish, or seal the bag, and refrigerate it for 12 to 24 hours.

Remove the chicken from the marinade, and discard the marinade. Mix the flour and cornstarch together in a shallow dish or bowl and toss the wings in this mixture until well coated on all sides.

Heat oil in a deep fryer to 375 degrees F.

Cook the wings until they are crispy brown and cooked through, and the juices run clear, 4 to 5 minutes.

Drain the chicken on paper towels and serve.

SERVES 8

SPICY "FRYED" GOBBLER STRIPS

1 (3- to 4-pound) turkey breast

MARINADE

1 tablespoon Heinz chili sauce

1 teaspoon Mexene chili powder

2 teaspoons rice wine

2 teaspoons soy sauce

1 teaspoon powdered ginger

1 tablespoon finely chopped green onions

1 teaspoon brown sugar

FLOUR COATING

⅔ cup flour

1 teaspoon paprika

1 tablespoon poultry seasoning

Oil for frying

On a cutting board, with a sharp knife, cut the turkey breast into strips, 3 inches long by 1 inch wide by ½ inch thick.

In a large bowl, mix the marinade ingredients well. Add the turkey strips and stir well to make sure each strip is covered. Marinate the strips for 1 hour at room temperature.

While the turkey is marinating, mix the flour, paprika, and poultry seasoning in a wide flat bowl or pan and set aside.

After the hour is up, Heat the oil in a Dutch oven or deep frying pot to 350 degrees F.

Remove the strips from the marinade and drain well over the bowl. Heat the remaining marinade in a small saucepan over high heat until it has boiled for 12 minutes. Take the pan off the heat, cool the marinade, and pour it into a sauceboat to serve at the table.

Lightly roll the turkey strips in the flour mixture. Using tongs, or a slotted spatula, slip the turkey strips into the hot oil and deep-fry them until they brown on all sides, about 8 minutes.

Remove the strips and drain them on paper towels. Serve at once on a heated platter with marinade on the side.

SERVES 4 TO 6

THAT'S JUST DUCKY!

MARINADE

1 cup shredded scallions

2 tablespoons mirin rice
   wine vinegar

2 tablespoons white wine

1 tablespoon shredded fresh
   ginger

½ cup soy sauce

½ teaspoon ground cloves

½ teaspoon coarse salt

½ teaspoon ground cinnamon

5 teaspoons ground
   Szechuan peppercorns

2 tablespoons hoisin sauce

1 (5- to 6-pound) duck,
   thawed, washed, and
   dried

Oil for frying

Measure the amount of oil you'll need to cook the duck using the water displacement method so oil doesn't overflow onto the flames (see page 4).

In a large bowl, mix together the marinade ingredients. Rub the mixture into the skin and body cavity of the duck. Cover the bowl with plastic wrap, place it in the refrigerator, and let the duck marinate overnight.

About an hour before cooking, remove the duck from the refrigerator, drain it well, pat the skin dry, and let the duck come to room temperature.

Place the duck in a steamer over high heat for 4 hours, replenishing the water as needed.

About 20 minutes before the 4 hours are up, heat the oil in a deep frying pot to 375 degrees F.

Remove the duck from the steamer, drain it, and pat the skin dry.

Carefully lower the duck in a fryer basket, or on a poultry hook, into the hot oil. Deep-fry it until it is brown all over, 10 to 15 minutes. Carefully lift the fryer basket or poultry hook and remove the duck from the hot oil. Use a meat thermometer to check the temperature of the bird, which should be 130 degrees F (for rare).

Drain thoroughly, and cut the duck into serving-size pieces, disjointing the legs and wings, and cutting the breast into at least 4 sections. Serve with warm hoisin sauce to dip.

SERVES 4 TO 6

SOUTHERN DEEP-FRIED CHICKIN'

2 eggs, beaten

1 cup heavy cream

1 cup stale beer

2 cups all-purpose flour

1 cup potato flour

2 teaspoons garlic salt

1 teaspoon white pepper

4 pounds of chicken
   parts (breasts,
   thighs, wings, and
   legs), washed and
   dried

Oil for frying

Preheat the oil in a deep fryer to 375 degrees F.

In a wide, flat bowl, mix the eggs, cream, and beer and lightly whip the liquid until foam appears. Set aside. In a plastic bag, mix the flours, garlic salt, and pepper.

Dip each piece of chicken into the egg mixture, then drop them into the plastic bag with the flour mixture and shake well to coat the chicken. Remove the coated chicken to a plate and continue until all the chicken has been coated.

Slip 3 or 4 chicken pieces at a time into the fryer and cook until golden, 8 to 10 minutes. Be sure to cook a small batch at a time so the pieces don't touch each other in the hot oil. Set a platter in an oven heated to 200 degrees F to keep the fried chicken pieces warm while you finish cooking all the chicken.

Remove the chicken from the oil with tongs or a slotted spoon and drain on paper towels. Serve immediately.

SERVES 4

CB's "TURDUCKEN" MEATBALLS

I KNOW, I KNOW: "TUR" IS SHORT FOR TURKEY, "DUCK" STANDS FOR (NO DUH!) DUCK, AND "EN" STANDS FOR CHICKEN. BUT YOU TRY FINDING GROUND DUCK IN THE SUPERMARKET. IF YOU CAN, GREAT. OR IF YOU HAVE DUCK BREASTS YOU CAN GRIND, GREAT. OTHERWISE BEEF IS GREAT, TOO. BUT "TURBURGEN" SOUNDS TOO WEIRD EVEN FOR THIS COOKBOOK. I WON'T TELL YOUR GUESTS IF YOU DON'T.

½ pound ground turkey

½ pound ground duck, or, if you can't find duck, ½ pound ground beef

½ pound ground chicken

½ cup bread crumbs

1 egg, beaten

1 cup finely minced onion

1 teaspoon granulated garlic

½ teaspoon Louisiana hot sauce

¼ teaspoon lemon pepper

½ teaspoon coarse salt

COATING

3 eggs, beaten

3 tablespoons half and half or milk

2 cups seasoned bread crumbs

1 teaspoon whole dried summer savory leaves

1 teaspoon paprika

Oil for frying

Preheat the oil in a deep fryer to 375 degrees F.

In a large bowl, combine the turkey, duck (or beef), chicken, bread crumbs, egg, onion, garlic, hot sauce, pepper, and salt. Mix with clean hands until combined. Use a teaspoon to measure the mixture into individual piles. Form the piles into 1- to 1½-inch meatballs. Refrigerate until needed.

To make the coating, in a wide, flat bowl, combine the eggs and the half and half and whip until just frothy. In another flat bowl, combine the bread crumbs, savory, and paprika.

Dip each meatball into the egg batter, then roll in breadcrumbs to coat evenly. Slip them 5 or 6 at a time into the hot oil and fry until golden brown, about 3 minutes. Remove from the hot oil with a slotted spoon and drain briefly on paper towels. Serve warm with toothpicks and a favorite barbecue or hoisin sauce for dipping.

SERVES 4 TO 6

NO. 4

RK & BEEF

NO. 4

PORK & BEEF

ANNE'S JALISCO MEAT PIES WITH CHEESE

2 cups flour

2 teaspoons baking powder

1 teaspoon salt

6 teaspoons cold shortening

8 tablespoons ice water

MEAT FILLING

1 pound lean ground pork

¼ pound olives stuffed with pimentos, chopped

1 teaspoon salt

2 tablespoons recaito (Goya brand)

½ teaspoon dried oregano

½ teaspoon black pepper

4 ounces tomato sauce

Grated cheddar cheese

1 egg, beaten

Oil for frying

Sift the flour into a bowl with the baking powder and salt. Add the shortening to the flour mixture and with a dough blender or a fork blend together, working very fast.

Add the water 1 tablespoon at a time, mixing well. Flour a flat surface and place the dough on top of it. Using your palms knead the dough very well until smooth. Form it into a ball and cover it with a moist towel to sit for 30 minutes.

While you are waiting, start your meat filling: Brown the ground pork in a medium skillet over high heat. Add all of the other filling ingredients, stir well, and cook for 15 to 20 minutes, until the meat is well browned. Remove the filling from the heat and let it cool.

Heat oil in a deep fryer to 375 degrees F.

Roll the chilled dough with your hands into a long roll on a floured board. The roll should be about 14 inches long. Cut off small 1- to 1½-inch lengths and with a rolling pin roll out these pieces of dough so they're very thin, about ⅛ inch in thickness.

Put some of the grated cheese and meat in the middle and fold over one side so that the cheese and meat are covered. Brush the edges with the beaten egg and seal them with a fork, making sure there are no openings. Put each pork turnover you make on a floured piece of aluminum foil while you finish the other pastries.

Put them into the fryer and start basting them with the hot oil immediately, or hold them gently under the hot oil, until they begin to inflate. Fry until golden brown on both sides, 3 to 4 minutes. Drain them on absorbent towels. Serve very warm.

SERVES 6 TO 8

BAXTER'S CHICKEN-FRIED STEAK

1 pound top round steak, trimmed
      (½ inch thick), cut in 4 pieces
1 cup buttermilk
1 teaspoon Louisiana hot sauce
1 cup flour
1 teaspoon salt, plus more to
      taste
1 tablespoon paprika
1 tablespoon garlic granules
½ teaspoon freshly ground
      pepper, plus more to taste
2 cups whole milk

Oil for frying

Using the flat side of a wooden kitchen mallet, pound the steaks to ¼ inch thick. Set them aside.

In a cast-iron Dutch oven, pour in oil to a depth of 2 to 3 inches and heat the oil to 375 degrees F.

In a small bowl, mix the buttermilk and hot sauce. In a medium bowl, combine the flour, 1 teaspoon salt, paprika, garlic, and ½ teaspoon pepper and mix well.

Put the steaks in a paper bag, add the seasoned flour, and shake to coat each piece of meat. Then dip each steak in the buttermilk mixture, then back into the bag with the flour mixture a second time.

Reserve 1½ tablespoons of the remaining flour mixture and set it aside. Heat the oven to 200 degrees F.

Deep-fry the steaks, two at a time, turning once, until golden brown on both sides, 2½ to 3 minutes. Using a slotted spatula, or a long pair of tongs, transfer the meat to a warm oven while making the gravy.

Carefully drain off all but 1½ tablespoons of the oil from the Dutch oven—it's still very hot. Over very low heat whisk in the reserved flour mixture and cook for 1 minute. Whisk in the milk and bring it to a simmer for approximately 3 minutes.

Remove the gravy from the heat and season with salt and pepper to taste. Serve the steak immediately, with the gravy on the side in a sauce dish.

SERVES 4

DEEP-FRIED SPARERIBS

1 whole slab pork ribs

RUB

¼ cup granulated garlic

¼ cup paprika

¼ cup seasoned salt

¼ cup lemon pepper

2 cups flour

2 cups yellow cornmeal

Oil for frying

Hold the slab of ribs upright in a horizontal position and using a sharp knife separate one rib from the slab by cutting right up against the bone. You now have a rib with meat on one side still attached to the slab. Take your knife and move over one rib so that you cut up against the second rib, thereby giving you a rib with meat on both sides. You get fewer rib bones, but each one has more meat on each side. Repeat on the remaining ribs, leaving all of the meat on one side of every second rib.

In a small bowl, mix the rub ingredients well. Take the individual ribs and rub them with ½ of the rib mix. Let the seasoned ribs sit at room temperature for about an hour. (The ribs will become tacky.)

Mix the flour and the cornmeal. Add the rest of the rub ingredients and roll each rib in the mixture.

Heat the oil in a 28- or 30-quart frying pot to 350 degrees F. Place the ribs in a frying basket, *turn off the gas*, and *slowly* lower the ribs into the hot oil.

Turn on the gas and cook the ribs for approximately 15 minutes or until they are golden brown.

Turn off the gas while you slowly remove the frying basket of ribs from the pot.

Drain on paper towels, and then serve with your favorite barbecue sauce on the side.

SERVES 2 TO 4

FRY-GRILLED PORK TENDERLOIN

Salt and pepper to taste

3 pounds pork tenderloin

RUB

1 teaspoon dried rosemary

1 teaspoon garlic powder

1 teaspoon seasoned salt

1 teaspoon lemon pepper

1 teaspoon ground ginger

1 teaspoon chili powder

MARINADE

12 ounces black cherry soda

⅔ cup packed brown sugar

½ cup soy sauce

¼ cup lemon juice

⅔ cup plum jam

4 tablespoons butter

Oil for frying

Heat the oil in a deep fryer or Dutch oven to 400 degrees F.

Salt and pepper the tenderloin and deep-fry it in hot oil for 3 minutes until well browned. Remove, drain, and cool to room temperature.

In a medium bowl, combine the rub ingredients and rub the mixture into the warm meat. Refrigerate the tenderloin overnight.

Combine the soda, brown sugar, soy sauce, lemon juice, and jam in a small saucepan over low heat; cook until well combined. Whisk in the butter to finish the marinade.

Bring the meat to room temperature, place it in a Ziploc bag and pour ⅓ of the marinade over the meat. Seal the bag and marinate for 1 to 2 hours in the refrigerator. Turn once or twice during that time. Drain the meat and discard the used marinade. Bring the meat to room temperature.

Oil the grate on a barbecue grill. Heat the barbecue grill to high heat (500 to 600 degrees). Place the tenderloin on it. Immediately turn the heat down to medium and grill the tenderloin for 10 to 15 minutes, turning 2 to 3 times. Baste often with ½ of the reserved marinade, making sure the meat doesn't burn due to the sugar content of marinade. Boil the remaining marinade in a medium saucepan for 10 minutes, remove from heat, cool, and put in a sauce boat.

Cover the meat in foil and let it rest for 5 minutes. Slice it into ¼-inch-thick medallions and serve it with the hot marinade sauce.

SERVES 6 TO 8

GOLDEN STATE OVERSTUFFED PEPPERS

3 golden bell peppers

FILLING

6 ounces ground pork

6 ounces ground turkey

½ teaspoon chopped fresh
   garlic

½ teaspoon chopped fresh
   ginger

1 teaspoon lemon salt

1 teaspoon mesquite powder

1 teaspoon Mexene chili
   powder

1 tablespoon balsamic
   vinegar

3 eggs, separated

1 cup plus 1 tablespoon flour

½ teaspoon cornstarch

Lettuce for garnish

Oil for frying

Heat oil to 360 degrees F in a Dutch oven or deep frying pot.

Cut the peppers in quarters lengthwise. Seed and wash them. Set aside.

In a large bowl, mix the ground pork and turkey with the garlic, ginger, salt, mesquite powder, chili powder, balsamic vinegar, and half of the egg whites. Set the filling aside.

With a wire whisk, in a wide flat bowl or pan, beat the rest of the egg whites with the yolks and mix with 1 tablespoon flour, the cornstarch, and enough water to make a thick batter.

Fill each quarter pepper with the filling, making sure it's level with the cut edges. Smooth the filling with a spatula or spoon and roll the peppers in the remaining 1 cup flour in a wide pan or bowl. Then dip the peppers, filling side down, into the batter, completely coating the filling.

With a slotted spoon slip the pepper quarters into the hot oil and deep-fry until the coating is golden brown, 2 to 3 minutes. Remove the peppers with a slotted spoon and drain them well on paper towels. When drained, arrange on lettuce and serve.

SERVES 4 TO 6

Hungry cowgals and cowpokes belly up to a delicious buffet, including deep-fried spareribs, in the Damnifino tent at the World's Bar-B-Que Championship in Houston, Texas.

Quebec French Fries

Deep-frying a turkey

Don't try this without reading all the safety tips, or you might end up like the guy on page 11!

Pitchfork Steaks

Hungarian Plums

Lime Crullers

Santa Maria Breakfast Biscuits

Citrus-y Churros

Fried Ice Cream
The balls of ice cream are frozen solid before they are rolled in the egg and then in the cornflake mixture.

Fry only one of the ice cream balls at a time to prevent them from melting.

The process is repeated so the ice cream balls don't melt during frying, and so they hold a nice coating for a lovely golden-brown crust!

Garnish them to your heart's delight and enjoy!

Hungarian Cherries

MAYUMI'S TEMPURA PORK CHOPS

SERVE WITH TERIYAKI SAUCE OR 2 CUPS APPLESAUCE SPICED WITH 1 TEASPOON RICE VINEGAR, ¼ TEASPOON GROUND CLOVES, AND ½ TEASPOON GROUND CINNAMON.

4 pork chops
½ teaspoon salt
¼ teaspoon pepper
¼ cup flour
1 egg, beaten
½ cup bread crumbs

Oil for frying

Heat 2 to 3 inches oil in a Dutch oven to 360 degree F.

Cut several vertical slits into the fat along the edges of the pork chops, to prevent chops from curling while cooking. Sprinkle a little salt and pepper on the chops.

Put the flour in a plastic bag, add the remaining salt and pepper, and add one pork chop, shaking the bag until it's covered. Dip both sides of the floured pork chop into the beaten egg in a shallow dish. Coat the chop with bread crumbs in another flat dish, and pat the chop to firmly set the crumb coating. Repeat for all the chops.

Fry the pork chops in the hot oil for a few minutes until one side turns brown, 2 to 3 minutes. Turn the chop over and cook the other side until brown.

Remove the chops from the hot oil with tongs and put them on a paper towel to drain.

SERVES 4

NIGHTSHADE RANCH COW PIES

CRUST

½ teaspoon salt

4 cups self-rising flour

2 eggs

1½ cups milk

½ cup Crisco

MEAT MIX

3 tablespoons plus 1 teaspoon
   vegetable oil

2 tablespoons flour

1 large onion, chopped

½ red or yellow bell pepper, chopped

1½ pounds ground chuck

1½ pounds pork sausage

1 tablespoon Louisiana hot sauce

⅛ teaspoon cayenne pepper

½ teaspoon garlic salt

1 clove garlic, chopped

1 teaspoon chopped fresh cilantro

½ teaspoon brown sugar

1 teaspoon Worcestershire sauce

Paprika for sprinkling

Oil for frying

To make the crust, blend the salt into the flour in a medium bowl, and add the eggs and milk. Cut in the Crisco and blend it with a fork until the flour looks slightly crumbly. Then form dough into a ball and refrigerate for at least 1 hour.

Dump the dough onto a clean floured countertop or cutting board and roll it to ¼-inch thickness. Fold the dough onto itself twice, and then roll it out again, this time to ⅛-inch thickness. Cut out 6-inch circles, then reroll the leftover dough and cut another batch of circles from it. Repeat until all the dough is used. Refrigerate the circles, covered with wax paper or plastic wrap, while you make the filling.

Heat 3 tablespoons of the oil and the flour together in a heavy, large cast-iron skillet. Cook over medium heat, stirring constantly, to make a medium-brown roux. Add the onion when the color is right, and sauté the onion until it begins to brown slightly, then add the bell pepper and cook for another 2 to 3 minutes.

Add the ground chuck and pork, hot sauce, cayenne, and salt. Break up the meat into small crumbles and cook until it is no longer pink. Remove the meat from heat and drain it in a large colander.

Heat the remaining 1 teaspoon oil in a large skillet over high heat. When a drop of water dropped in the skillet sizzles, it is the right temperature. Add the garlic, cilantro, brown sugar, and Worcestershire, cook for 1 to 2 minutes until the garlic just starts to color, then add the drained meat mixture and cook for another 8 to 10 minutes or so, stirring now and then to keep the meat from clumping, until the meat is well browned.

Transfer the meat mixture to a clean colander to drain and cool for a few minutes. Put the meat in a container, cover, and refrigerate it overnight. The next day, bring it to room temperature to make the pies.

On a floured surface take a dough circle and place a generous serving-spoon-sized amount of filling onto one half of the circle. Moisten the edge of the circle with a little water, and fold the unfilled half over into a half-moon, then press down the edges with a fork to seal them, so that a pocket is formed around the filling. Repeat with remaining circles.

Heat the oil in a deep fryer to 350 degrees F.

Fry 1 to 3 pies at a time, until golden brown, 4 to 5 minutes, making sure the temperature has returned to 350 degrees as you start each batch, since the temperature may fall due to the introduction of solids.

Drain the pies and sprinkle them with paprika. Serve them warm or hot.

SERVES 18 TO 24

OLD SMOKEY'S HAM BALLS WITH JAMBON SAUCE

2 smoked pork chops, finely chopped, about ½ pound

1 pound smoked ham, finely chopped

1 pound ground pork or turkey

2 cups seasoned bread crumbs

3 large eggs, beaten

1 large sweet onion, minced

¼ cup finely chopped green onions, green tops only

1 teaspoon chopped fresh parsley

1 tablespoon firmly packed brown sugar

2 teaspoons dry mustard

1 teaspoon seasoned salt

Pepper to taste

½ cup light cream, or half and half

1 tablespoon Steen's cane syrup, or molasses

Dash of Louisiana hot sauce

Lettuce for garnish

Jambon Sauce (recipe follows)

Oil for frying

In a large bowl, combine the pork chops, ham, ground pork or turkey, bread crumbs, eggs, onion, green onions, parsley, brown sugar, mustard, salt, and pepper. Add the cream, cane syrup, and hot sauce. With a large spoon mix well and refrigerate, in a covered bowl, for at least 20 minutes.

Remove from the refrigerator and shape into 1- to 2-inch balls. When all the mixture has been used up you should have close to 40 ham balls. Refrigerate in a covered dish for a minimum of 1 hour. Longer is better, up to 4 hours.

Heat the oil in the deep fryer to 375 degrees.

Remove the meat from the refrigerator and using a large slotted spoon transfer the ham balls to the hot oil, frying in batches, until the balls are crispy brown and cooked through, 3 to 4 minutes.

Drain them on paper towels. Serve the ham balls on a bed of lettuce on a large platter. Accompany with Jambon Sauce.

SERVES 8 TO 10

Jambon Sauce

1 (18-ounce) jar crabapple
  jelly

1 (18-ounce) jar mint jelly

4 tablespoons prepared
  mustard

½ teaspoon ground cinnamon

½ teaspoon ground nutmeg

1 tablespoon black pepper

Dash of Louisiana jalapeño
  hot sauce

In a small saucepan, combine all the ingredients and heat over medium heat until well combined and smooth. Remove the pan from heat and pour the sauce into a glass bottle. Cover and chill until ready to serve. Warm to room temperature and put in a saucepan to serve alongside the ham balls.

MAKES 4 CUPS

PEDERNALES RIVER BEEF SHORT RIBS

2 to 2½ pounds beef short ribs

3 green onions, chopped in 1-inch pieces

2 cloves garlic, mashed

½ teaspoon minced fresh ginger root

3 tablespoons Steen's cane syrup

2 teaspoons brown sugar

1 teaspoon seasoned salt

2 tablespoons olive oil

3 (12-ounce) bottles beer

BATTER

2 eggs

½ cup cornstarch

1 teaspoon garlic salt

1 teaspoon black pepper

Dash of Louisiana hot sauce

Oil for frying

With a sharp meat cleaver, chop the ribs into 2-inch lengths. Place them in a large stockpot or Dutch oven. Add the green onions, garlic, ginger, cane syrup, brown sugar, salt, olive oil, and beer to the pot. If the ribs are not covered, add cold water until they are completely under liquid. Bring the ribs to a boil over high heat, then lower the heat, cover the pot, and simmer for 1 hour.

Heat the oil in Dutch oven or deep pot fryer to 375 degrees F.

Drain the ribs in a colander, reserving 1 cup of the cooking liquid. Let the ribs cool.

Beat the eggs lightly and blend with the cornstarch to a make a smooth batter. Thin it slightly with some of the reserved beef stock. Add the salt, pepper, and hot sauce. Using tongs, dip the ribs into the batter to coat them completely.

Using long tongs add ribs, 2 to 3 at a time, to the hot oil and deep-fry them until they are golden on both sides, 3 to 4 minutes.

Remove the ribs with tongs, drain them on paper towels, and serve on a heated platter with your favorite BBQ sauce on the side.

SERVES 4 TO 6

PITCHFORK STEAKS

WARNING: A PITCHFORK HAS THREE TINES THAT ARE SLIGHTLY CURVED, A MANURE FORK HAS FOUR TINES THAT ARE ALMOST STRAIGHT. BE CAREFUL WHICH ONE YOU BUY TO COOK ON. "PITCHFORK STEAKS" SOUNDS EXOTIC AND FUN, MANURE FORK STEAKS SOUNDS, WELL, LESS THAN APPETIZING.

4 (1-pound) rib-eye steaks

4 tablespoons olive oil

2 tablespoons McCormick Montreal
    steak seasoning

4 pats butter

Oil for frying

Heat the oil in a deep fryer to 385 degrees F.

Rub each of the steaks with 1 tablespoon of olive oil, then sprinkle generously with the Montreal steak seasoning.

Take a brand-new pitchfork and skewer all 4 steaks on the tines.

Dip the pitchfork in the hot oil for 2½ minutes (medium rare) to 3½ minutes (medium).

Remove the steaks to sizzling platters and serve them immediately. Put a pat of butter on each steak on the platter and let it melt into the meat and mingle with the juices.

SERVES 4

YOU-AIN'T-GONNA-BELIEVE-THIS PRIME RIB

2 teaspoons kosher salt

2 teaspoons citrus flavored
    black pepper

2 teaspoons chopped fresh
    rosemary

1 (6- to 8-pound) prime rib

5 cloves garlic, slivered

Sprig of fresh parsley or
    rosemary for garnish

Fried Onions (recipe
    follows)

3 gallons peanut oil
    for frying

The night before you plan to serve your prime rib, mix the salt, pepper, and rosemary and rub the meat with it liberally. Using a small knife make shallow cuts all over the roast, then insert slivers of garlic into the cuts. Cover the meat and place it in the refrigerator overnight.

Remove the roast from the refrigerator and bring it to room temperature (1 to 1½ hours).

Heat the oil to 365 degrees F in a turkey pot with a hook and stand or a boiling basket.

Turn off the gas, then slowly lower the prime rib into the oil. You can expect the oil to drop in temperature quickly, probably down to approximately 330 degrees F. Turn the gas back on and heat up the burner to bring the temperature back up to 365 degrees F, then level off the heat as you reach the correct temperature.

Cook the prime rib for 3 minutes per pound of weight for medium-rare (18 to 24 minutes), 4 minutes per pound for medium (24 to 32 minutes).

Turn off the gas and, using the frying basket or tongs, carefully remove the prime rib from the hot oil and let it rest, covered with aluminum foil, for 10 to 15 minutes on a broiling pan.

Slice and serve the meat on a heated platter garnished with sprigs of fresh parsley or rosemary and fried onions.

SERVES 8 TO 10

Fried Onions

1 dozen boiling onions,
    peeled with root trimmed
    (1 to 1½ inches)
Brown sugar for sprinkling
Pinch of garlic salt
Fresh ground pepper to taste

After the prime rib has been removed, use a slotted spoon to remove any large particles floating in the oil.

Then, using a slotted spoon, slip the onions into the 365-degree oil and cook till brown, 2 to 3 minutes, turning with a wooden spoon to cook evenly.

Remove the onions from the pan with a slotted spoon, and quickly drain them on paper towels. Transfer the onions to a small saucepan over medium-high heat, and sprinkle them with brown sugar, and salt and pepper to taste. Cook them until the sugar starts to caramelize, 4 to 5 minutes, then serve the onions alongside prime rib or beef roast.

SERVES 8 TO 10

STATE FAIR CORN DOGS

1 cup flour

1 cup cornmeal

1 tablespoon sugar

1 tablespoon
   baking powder

1 teaspoon salt

Dash of pepper

2 eggs

1 cup milk

¼ cup vegetable oil

1 pound hot dogs

Oil for frying

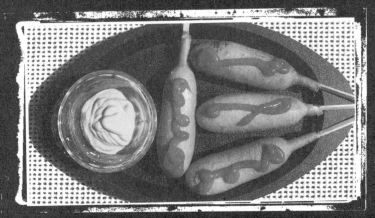

In a large bowl, add the flour, cornmeal, sugar, baking powder, salt, and pepper, and stir the ingredients together. In a medium bowl beat the eggs with milk and add ¼ cup oil. Pour this mixture into the flour mixture and whisk them together until the batter is smooth. Let the batter sit for 20 minutes to firm it up. It should be very thick to coat the dogs evenly.

Heat oil in a deep fryer to 360 degrees F.

Insert a popsicle stick into the end of each hot dog. Using the stick as a handle, dip each hot dog into batter and turn to coat it evenly. Fry several corn dogs at a time, making sure they don't stick together, until golden, 3 to 5 minutes. Drain on paper towels. Serve with yellow mustard and ketchup.

SERVES 4 TO 8

CHRIS'S CHICKEN-FRIED CHOPS

½ cup all-purpose flour

1 teaspoon ground yellow mustard

1 teaspoon granulated garlic

½ teaspoon mesquite smoke powder (see Note)

1 teaspoon salt

1 teaspoon lemon pepper

6 pork loin chops, about ¾ inch thick

Oil for frying

Preheat the oil in deep fryer to 400 degrees F.

In a wide, shallow bowl, combine the flour, mustard, garlic, mesquite smoke powder, salt, and lemon pepper and stir well. Reserve half of this mixture.

Dredge the chops in one half of the dry mixture, coating well. Place 2 or 3 chops in a deep-fryer basket and slowly lower it into the hot oil. Cook for 2½ to 3 minutes or until the chops are browned and curl slightly. Remove the chops from the oil and drain them briefly on paper towels.

Just before serving, sprinkle the chops lightly with the remaining dry mixture and serve them on a very hot platter.

SERVES 6

Note: Available on-line from www.oregonspice.com.

PERSIAN LAMB DUMPLINGS

YOU CAN OFTEN FIND DUMPLING ROUNDS AT YOUR LOCAL GROCERY STORE IN THE ASIAN FOOD SECTION, SO YOU DON'T HAVE TO MAKE THEM YOURSELF.

DOUGH

4 cups flour

1 teaspoon salt

3 eggs

1 cup cold water

FILLING

3 tablespoons butter

1 tablespoon olive oil

¾ pound finely ground lamb

1 teaspoon minced garlic

3 tablespoons minced onion

2 eggs, beaten

2 tablespoons finely chopped
   mint

2 tablespoons finely chopped
   cilantro

3 tablespoons cold cooked rice

1 teaspoon salt

1 teaspoon white pepper

Oil for deep-frying

To make the dough, combine the flour and salt in a shallow bowl. Add the eggs and water and work the dough into a ball with your hands. Remove the dough to a floured surface and roll it out with a floured rolling pin. Knead the dough by folding it in half lengthwise, then rolling it out, folding it again, and repeating this process until the dough is elastic, 10 to 15 minutes. Sprinkle with flour as needed. Wrap the dough in plastic wrap and let stand at room temperature for 1 hour.

To make the filling, in a nonstick frying pan over high heat, melt the butter with the olive oil. Stir in the lamb, garlic, and onion and sauté until the meat is cooked through, about 5 minutes. Pour the meat mixture into a wide, shallow bowl. Remove and discard any fat left in the pan. Add the eggs, mint, cilantro, rice, salt, and pepper, and cook, mixing well with a large spoon. Add to the meat mixture and set aside to cool.

Preheat the oil in a deep fryer to 375 degrees F.

Remove the dough from the bowl and, on a floured board, using a floured rolling pin, roll out dough to ⅟₁₆-inch thickness. Using a large cookie cutter or a drinking glass, cut the dough into 3-inch rounds. The dough should yield about 12 rounds. Using your hands, stretch each round until it's almost paper-thin and about 4 to 4½ inches in diameter.

Place 1 teaspoon of lamb filling in the center of each dumpling round, then fold the filled circles of dough to make a half-moon shape. Seal them with your fingers and crimp the edges with a fork dipped in cold water.

Slip 2 or 3 dumplings at a time into the hot oil with a slotted spoon and cook until golden brown, about 3 minutes. Remove from the oil and drain on paper towels. Serve with rice or cottage-fried potatoes.

SERVES 6

NO. 5

FISH & SHELLFISH

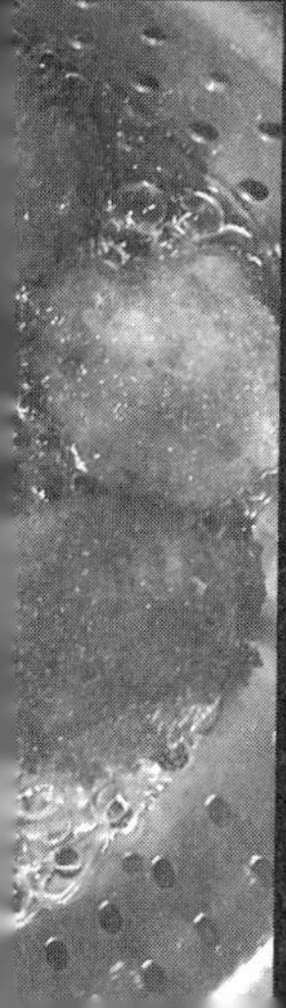

NO. 5

FISH & SHELLFISH

BAJA-STYLE FISH BITES

1¼ cups corn chips

MARINADE

⅓ cup sour cream

1 tablespoon lime juice

½ teaspoon Mexene chili
   powder

2 tablespoons butter, melted

1 pound red snapper fillets

1 cup flour

Oil for frying

Heat the oil in a Dutch oven or deep fryer pot to 375 degrees F.

Place the corn chips in a plastic bag, and using a rolling pin, crush them to a crumblike consistency. Pour the crumbs into a wide, flat bowl.

In a wide, flat bowl or baking dish, whisk or mix together the sour cream, lime juice, chili powder, and butter.

Cut the fish fillets into bite-sized (1- to 2-inch) pieces. In another flat pan dredge the fish pieces in the flour, covering all sides of the pieces evenly.

Soak the floured fish pieces in the marinade, again coating both sides well. Let the fish sit in the marinade for 1 to 2 minutes. Drain the excess marinade back into the bowl. Dredge the fish in the crushed corn chips, coating both sides well by pressing down on them with the back of a spoon while they are in the bowl.

Slip the pieces, no more than two at a time, into the hot oil and fry them until they are golden brown on both sides, 3 to 4 minutes.

Serve the fried fish pieces with a spicy tomato or fruit salsa on the side.

SERVES 4

BEER-BATTER TROUT

6 (¾ pound each) brook or
    rainbow trout

2 cups plus 2 to 3
    tablespoons flour

2 teaspoons baking powder

1 teaspoon salt

1 tablespoon mild curry
    powder

2 eggs, slightly beaten

2 cups warm beer

½ cup salad oil

Fresh parsley for garnish

Lemon slices for garnish

Oil for frying

Heat the oil in a deep fryer or Dutch oven to 375 degrees F.

Wash and pat the fish dry, then put them in a paper bag with 2 to 3 tablespoons of flour and shake until the fish are coated with flour. Set aside.

In a large bowl, combine the remaining 2 cups flour, the baking powder, salt, curry powder, eggs, beer, and salad oil; whisk until the mixture is smooth. Dip the floured fish into this batter, allowing the excess to drip back into the bowl.

Slip the fish into the oil and cook, turning once or twice, until golden brown on both sides, 3 to 4 minutes. Remove the fish from the oil with a slotted spatula or frying basket. Drain on paper towels. Garnish with fresh parsley and lemon slices.

SERVES 6

COCONUT-BATTERED SHRIMP

DIPPING SAUCE

4 ounces piña colada mix

6 tablespoons sour cream

¼ cup drained, crushed pineapple

3 pounds shrimp, uncooked

1¼ cups flour

1½ teaspoons baking powder

1½ teaspoons salt

1 tablespoon honey granules
   (see Note)

1 cup milk

1 egg

3 tablespoons butter, melted

1 cup shredded coconut

Oil for frying

Heat the oil in a deep fryer or Dutch oven to 350 degrees F.

Mix the dipping sauce ingredients in a glass or stainless steel bowl and set aside.

Shell, clean, and devein the shrimp, but leave the tails on. Butterfly each shrimp by cutting lengthwise almost all the way through.

Sift the flour, baking powder, and salt into a medium bowl. Add the honey granules, milk, egg, and melted butter. Whisk the mixture until smooth. Pour the coconut shreds into a wide, flat bowl or pan.

Holding the shrimp by their tails, dip them into the batter, let the excess drip off into the bowl, then roll the shrimp in the coconut to cover.

Deep-fry the shrimp until golden, 3 to 4 minutes. Using a frying basket or slotted spoon, remove them from the oil and drain on paper towels. Serve immediately with individual bowls of the dipping sauce.

SERVES 6 TO 8

Note: Available on-line at www.oregonspice.com.

DOVER CODFISH AND CHIPS

6 potatoes, approximately 1½ pounds

BATTER

½ teaspoon baking powder

1¼ cups flour

1 teaspoon salt plus more to taste

½ teaspoon white pepper

1 tablespoon vegetable oil

¾ cup beer

¼ cup light cream (or whole milk)

3 egg whites

1½ pounds cod fillets

Lemon wedges for garnish

Malt vinegar for dipping

Tartar sauce for dipping

Oil for frying

Peel the potatoes and square each end and sides, then cut each into ¾-inch slices. Stack and cut them into ¾-inch sticks. Place in a bowl of ice-cold water to soak for 30 minutes to crisp them up.

Sift the baking powder, flour, salt, and pepper into a large, wide bowl. Make a well in the middle of the flour, add the vegetable oil and beer, stir. Gradually add the cream (or milk) until well mixed. The batter will become elastic. Let the batter stand for 30 to 35 minutes, till thickened.

Heat the oil in a deep-fat fryer or Dutch oven to 350 degrees F. Heat the oven to 200 degrees F.

Drain the potatoes, pat *very* dry using paper towels. Dip an empty frying basket into the oil (this prevents potatoes from sticking to it), then add the potatoes, and lower the basket into the oil. Deep-fry the potatoes till just tender when pierced, and starting to brown, 3 to 4 minutes.

Lift the basket out of the oil and drain the potatoes in a basket or on a wire rack. They are now partially cooked.

In a copper bowl, whisk the egg whites till stiff peaks form. Gently fold the stiff whites into the rested batter, using a rubber spatula, until combined. Dip the cod fillets in the batter, turning to coat each piece thoroughly, and letting excess batter drip off into the bowl.

Using a slotted spatula, slide the fillets into the hot oil, turning once, frying 6 to 8 minutes until golden and crisp on the outside. Remove to a flat pan or baking sheet lined with paper towels, and keep the fillets warm in the oven as you fry the rest.

After the fish has been cooked, place the potatoes back in the fryer basket and fry them till golden brown, 1 to 2 minutes. Drain them on paper towels.

To serve, sprinkle the chips with salt and decorate the fish with lemon wedges. Serve with malt vinegar and tartar sauce on the side.

SERVES 6

FILLET-WRAPPED PRAWNS

**CHOOSE FLAT FILLETS OF FIRM WHITE FISH LIKE CATFISH OR SOLE. FILLETS SHOULD BE THIN,
FOR THEY HAVE TO BE ROLLED AROUND THE PRAWNS.**

1 pound firm white fish fillets

12 large prawns

BATTER

2 eggs, beaten

¼ teaspoon blackened seasoning

¼ teaspoon Louisiana hot sauce

½ teaspoon salt

BREADING

1 cup flour

1 cup bread crumbs

BBQ sauce or tartar sauce
    for dipping

Lemon wedges for garnish

Oil for frying

Heat the oil in a Dutch oven or deep frying pot to 350 degrees F.

Heat the oven to 200 degrees F.

Use a sharp knife to remove the skin from the fillets. Depending on the size of the fillets, they may then be cut into 2, 3, or 4 strips. You want strips that are at least 1 inch wide.

Shell the prawns and devein them. Wrap a fillet strip around each prawn and fasten it with a wooden toothpick.

Mix the beaten eggs with the blackened spices, hot sauce, and salt. Roll the wrapped prawns in the flour, then dip them into the egg mixture, and roll them gently into the bread crumbs.

Using a slotted spoon or spatula, slide the fish rolls, about 6 at a time, into the hot oil. Fry them until golden brown all over, approximately 3 minutes.

Remove them from the oil and drain on paper towels. Place on a cookie sheet in the warm oven while the rest of the rolls are cooking.

Serve hot with BBQ sauce or tartar sauce for dipping. Arrange lemon wedges on the side.

SERVES 6

HEAVENLY FRIED OYSTERS

½ cup flour

18 large, fresh oysters, shucked

2 eggs

4 tablespoons heavy cream

1 cup fine dry bread crumbs

2 tablespoons dried parsley

1 teaspoon garlic powder

1 teaspoon salt

1 teaspoon citrus pepper

Lemon wedges for garnish

Oil for frying

Heat the oil in a deep fryer or Dutch oven to 375 degrees F.

Put the flour in a paper bag. Drain the oysters, drop them into the paper bag, and shake them until coated with flour. Set them aside on a floured plate.

Beat the eggs and cream in a shallow bowl. Combine the bread crumbs, parsley, garlic powder, salt, and pepper in another shallow bowl. Dip the floured oysters in the cream and egg mixture, then roll in the bread crumb mixture, pressing down lightly on both sides to ensure a good coating of crumbs. (For a thicker coating, repeat the process.)

Fry about 6 at a time in the hot oil, 2 to 3 minutes, or until golden brown. Drain them on paper towels. Serve with the lemon wedges.

SERVES 4 TO 6

OL' KING COD

BATTER

1 egg

¾ cup flour

½ cup water

1 teaspoon salt

¼ teaspoon ground ginger

1 tablespoon sesame seeds

½ teaspoon paprika

1 pound cod fillets, frozen or fresh

Oil for frying

In a large bowl, mix the batter ingredients together and let them rest for 20 minutes to thicken.

Heat 1 inch of oil in a Dutch oven to 375 degrees F.

Thaw (if frozen) or rinse (if fresh) and pat dry the cod fillets. Cut them into serving-sized pieces and dip the pieces into the batter. Drain them briefly but make sure each piece is coated.

Deep-fry the fish for 4 to 5 minutes on each side or until golden brown.

SERVES 4

PEANUT-CORNMEAL FRIED CATFISH

1½ pounds catfish fillets,
    fresh or frozen

6 tablespoons ground peanuts

⅔ cup yellow cornmeal

¼ teaspoon salt

¼ teaspoon ground black
    pepper

¼ teaspoon ground red pepper

¼ cup milk

1 large egg, beaten

Oil for frying

Heat 2 inches of oil in a cast-iron Dutch oven or deep fryer to 375 degrees F. Heat the oven to 200 degrees F.

Rinse the fresh fish and pat fillets dry. If frozen, thaw and rinse, then pat dry. Cut the fillets into 6 equal-sized pieces.

In a wide, flat dish, combine the ground peanuts, cornmeal, salt, black pepper, and red pepper. In a similar dish, combine the milk and egg.

With your fingers dip each piece of fish in the milk mixture, then roll in the nut mixture. Use your hand or a wide spoon to gently press the nuts into the flesh.

Fry 1 or 2 pieces of fish at a time, about 2 minutes on each side, or until golden brown.

Carefully remove the fish with a slotted spoon and place fillets on paper towels to drain. Keep them warm in the oven while frying up the remaining fish.

SERVES 6

PHRIED LOBSTA

2 cups cornmeal

½ cup flour

1 teaspoon paprika

1 teaspoon garlic powder

1 teaspoon onion powder

½ teaspoon cayenne pepper

1 teaspoon lemon zest
   granules

Kosher salt to taste

Lemon pepper to taste

4 pounds lobster tails, halved
   and still in shell

Oil for frying

Heat the vegetable oil in a deep fryer or Dutch oven to 365 degrees F. Heat the oven to 200 degrees F.

In a 1-gallon Ziploc bag, combine the cornmeal, flour, paprika, garlic powder, onion powder, cayenne, lemon zest, salt, and pepper. Shake well to mix.

Drop 1 to 2 lobster tails into the bag one at a time and shake well, until each tail is well covered with spice mixture.

Slip one coated lobster tail at a time into the hot oil. Cook until the lobster meat turns white and the coating lightly browns. Remove lobster from oil with slotted spoon and put pieces on a paper-towel-covered pan in the warm oven to drain while the rest of the tails are cooking.

Serve lobster on a heated platter with individual bowls of melted lemon-butter. Use 1 teaspoon of lemon juice for every ¼ cup of butter.

SERVES 4 TO 6

SALT AND PEPPA SHRIMPS

1 pound (medium) shrimp

1 tablespoon vodka

1½ teaspoons salt

⅛ teaspoon white pepper

BATTER

1 cup flour

2 teaspoons baking powder

1 cup cold water

DIPPING SPICES

6 tablespoons kosher, or
   coarse sea salt

½ teaspoon black
   peppercorns

2 tablespoons Szechuan
   peppercorns

2 cups oil for frying

Heat the oil for in a deep fryer or Dutch oven to 350 degrees F.

Using your fingers, carefully remove the shells from the shrimp, leaving the tails intact. Devein and wash the shrimp under cold running water and then pat them dry with paper towels.

In a shallow glass or stainless steel bowl, marinate the shrimp for 10 to 15 minutes, in a mixture of the vodka, salt, and white pepper, turning frequently.

To make the batter put the flour and baking powder in a medium bowl and gradually add the cold water, mixing until smooth. Let the batter rest while you make the dipping spices. Combine salt and black and Szechuan peppercorns in a medium bowl, then pour this mixture into a dry skillet. Heat over high heat, stirring often, until the spices begin to brown, 4 to 5 minutes.

When browned, remove the spices with a spoon and pour into a pepper grinder or countertop pulse grinder. (In a pinch, you can use a clean coffee grinder, then remember to run some pieces of bread through the grinder so you don't have salty or peppery coffee the next time you use it.)

Take 1 tablespoon of the hot oil and mix it into the batter, stirring to combine the ingredients. Take the shrimp by their tails and dip them into the batter, leaving their tails unbattered. Gently lower the shrimp into the hot oil 5 or 6 at a time.

Deep-fry the shrimp until golden brown, about 2 minutes for each batch.

Remove from oil with a slotted spoon, drain on paper towels, and serve, tails up, in a shrimp serving dish or deep soup bowl. Put the ground pepper/salt mix in a small bowl and place on the table so guests can dip their shrimp into the fragrant spices.

SERVES 4

SCHWIMP AND KWAB WWAP

DOUGH

2 cups flour (unbleached preferred)

3 tablespoons oil

¾ cup water

Pinch of salt

FILLING

8 tablespoons oil

4 cloves garlic, minced

3 medium shallots, minced

¾ pound shrimp, chopped

¾ pound fresh crabmeat, shredded

1 medium onion, halved and finely
chopped

2 tablespoons chopped fresh parsley

1 tablespoon curry powder

1 teaspoon paprika

4 eggs

1 stalk green onion, finely sliced

Salt to taste

White pepper to taste

1 egg yolk

3 tablespoons milk

Oil for frying

In a large bowl, combine all the dough ingredients and knead them into an oily, elastic dough, about 10 minutes. Cover the dough with a moist towel and leave it at room temperature for 2 to 4 hours. Divide the dough into 4 pieces and roll each piece into a ball. Using lightly oiled hands on an oiled surface, pull the dough to form 4 large (6-inch diameter) circles. Evenly roll the circles flat with a rolling pin. Set aside the pieces to rest, covered, separated by layers of wax paper or aluminum foil.

While the dough is resting, make the filling. Heat the oil and sauté the garlic and shallots in a nonstick frying pan for a few seconds over medium-high heat. Do not let the garlic turn brown. Add the chopped shrimp and crab, and stir-fry over medium-high heat until the meat changes from translucent white to a solid white. Add the onion and fresh parsley and continue stir-frying for another 2 minutes. Add the curry powder and paprika, stir, and cook 3 minutes. Set aside to cool to room temperature.

After mixture has cooled add the 4 eggs, green onion, salt, and pepper to the mix, stir well, and then divide the cooked filling in four parts.

Lightly beat the yolk and the milk in a small bowl and set aside.

Heat the oil in a Dutch oven or deep fryer to 350 degrees F.

Place a thin circle of dough in the middle of a floured cutting board, and fill one side of the dough with one of the piles of the shrimp-crab filling. Spread evenly and then brush the edges with the egg yolk–milk mixture to seal. Fold in the sides and ends to completely enclose the filling, envelope fashion.

Fry the pastries until they are golden brown on one side, about 1 minute, then turn and brown the other side for about 1 minute. Remove from oil with a slotted spatula, then drain them on absorbent paper towels. Serve on a hot platter.

SERVES 4

WORLD'S BEST EATIN' SHARK
with Fresh Mango Salsa

2 pounds shark fillets (or
   haddock)

2 cups milk

BATTER

1 tablespoon butter

⅔ cup Hungry Jack biscuit
   mix

1 teaspoon salt

½ teaspoon granulated garlic

½ teaspoon chili powder

¼ teaspoon pepper

1 cup plus 2 tablespoons
   flour

Mango Salsa (recipe follows)

Oil for frying

Skin the fish and cut it into 3 by 5-inch pieces. Wash them under cold running water and then pat them completely dry with paper towels. In a shallow pan or baking dish, soak the fillets in milk for 2 to 4 hours in the refrigerator, drain, and discard the milk. Dry and pat dry the fillets.

Heat oil in a Dutch oven or frying pot to 375 degrees F.

Melt the butter in a small pan. Mix the remaining batter ingredients in a shallow baking dish, reserving 1 cup of the flour, and add the melted butter.

Put the shark fillets in a paper bag with 1 cup flour, and shake until coated.

Drop 2 or 3 pieces of the fish at a time into the batter until they are well coated. Using a spoon or spatula, slip them into the hot oil. Fry 4 to 5 minutes, or until golden brown, turning the pieces occasionally with a spoon to prevent their sticking together.

Serve with Mango Salsa.

SERVES 6 TO 8

Mango Salsa

- ¾ cup orange juice
- ⅛ teaspoon salt
- 3 tablespoons packed brown sugar
- 1½ cups diced mango, ¼ inch long
- ¼ bunch cilantro, chopped in large pieces
- 3 teaspoons seeded and minced jalapeño
- ½ teaspoon ground black pepper

In a medium saucepan over medium heat, reduce the orange juice, salt, and sugar by half. Remove from the heat and cool. When cooled, pour into a small bowl and add the mango, cilantro, jalapeño, and black pepper. Mix well and chill.

SERVES 6 TO 8

STUMPTOWN OYSTERS 'N' BACON

1 dozen shucked oysters (or if fresh not available, in a jar)

¼ cup oyster liquor, from jar

1 bay leaf

1 teaspoon Louisiana hot sauce

3 eggs, beaten

½ cup flour

1 teaspoon garlic

6 slices bacon

1 cup bread crumbs

Oil for frying

Heat oil in a Dutch oven or deep frying pot to 350 degrees F.

In a large saucepan over medium heat, poach the oysters in the oyster liquor, with the bay leaf and hot sauce, until the edges of the oysters curl, 1 to 1½ minutes. Remove the oysters from the liquor and set them aside. Discard the cooking liquid.

Put the eggs and flour in separate wide, flat bowls. Add granulated garlic to the flour and stir well.

Cut the bacon strips in half lengthwise. Wrap each oyster with a strip of bacon and fasten it with a wooden toothpick. Roll the bacon-wrapped oysters in the flour, dip them in the egg mixture, and then roll them in the bread crumbs.

Slip the oysters into the deep fryer and cook until the bacon and oysters are browned and golden, 4 to 5 minutes.

Remove the cooked oysters with a slotted spoon and drain them on paper towels. Serve on a hot platter.

SERVES 2 TO 4

SHRIMPCAKES ARE A-COMIN'

**THESE ARE DELICIOUS SERVED WITH A FRESH FRUIT SALSA OR SOUR CREAM
FLAVORED WITH CURRY, GREEN ONION, OR LEMON.**

4 cups prepared instant
mashed potatoes, cooled

2 cups small shrimp, drained
and chopped

4 eggs

2 tablespoons favorite
barbecue sauce

Dash of Louisiana hot sauce
(or Tabasco)

Dash of Worcestershire
sauce

3 tablespoons minced green
onion

½ teaspoon curry powder

Salt and pepper to taste

Flour for dusting

2 tablespoons heavy cream
or half and half

¼ cup seasoned bread
crumbs

¼ cup crushed Ritz crackers
(or your favorite cracker)

Oil for frying

Place the mashed potatoes in a medium bowl.

Chop the shrimp into pieces the size of the tip of your little finger and add to the mashed potatoes. In a small bowl, beat 2 eggs. Add them to the shrimp mixture along with the barbecue sauce, hot sauce, Worcestershire, green onion, curry powder, and salt and pepper. Stir until well mixed. Refrigerate for 2 to 3 hours to let the mixture firm and set.

Remove the shrimpcake mixture from the refrigerator and divide into 8 equal portions. Flour your hands lightly, then shape the 8 portions into individual patties, which will be about 1 inch thick and about 3 inches in diameter.

In a wide, flat bowl, beat the remaining 2 eggs and the cream until frothy and set them aside. In another wide, flat bowl, mix the bread crumbs and crackers.

Dip each patty into the egg–cream mixture, then into the bread crumb mixture to coat evenly and well. Refrigerate the patties for 30 to 45 minutes to allow them to set properly.

Preheat the oil in a deep fryer to 375 degrees F.

Slip the patties, 3 or 4 at a time, into the hot oil and fry until golden on both sides, 3 to 4 minutes. Remove from the oil with a slotted spoon and drain on paper towels.

SERVES 4 TO 8

SANTA CRUZ BOARDWALK CALAMARI

IF YOU'RE A SHARP COOKIE, YOU'LL BUY THE CALAMARI (SQUID) ALREADY CUT AT YOUR GROCERY STORE, BUTCHER SHOP, OR FISHMONGER. (WHAT IS A MONGER, ANYWAY?) IF YOU HAVE FRESH SQUID, YOU ARE ON YOUR OWN. I WOULDN'T HAVE A CLUE HOW TO CLEAN THEM, NOR WOULD I WISH TO. YEECCH.

1 cup flour

1 tablespoon whole dried summer savory leaves

1 tablespoon garlic powder

1 teaspoon salt

½ teaspoon white pepper

2 eggs, beaten

2 tablespoons cream or half and half

1½ pounds fresh or frozen squid, cut into ½- to 1-inch rings plus small tentacles

Lemon wedges for garnish

Fresh parsley for garnish

Oil for frying

Preheat the oil in a deep fryer to 350 degrees F.

In a large, flat bowl combine the flour, savory, garlic powder, salt, and white pepper, and stir well. In another flat bowl, beat together the eggs and cream until slightly frothy.

Dip each piece of calamari into the flour mix, then into the beaten egg, then back again into the flour so that each piece is well coated with batter.

With a frying basket or a slotted spoon, slip the calamari, 6 to 8 pieces at a time, into the hot oil and cook until golden, 2½ to 3 minutes. Cook the rings first, then the tentacles, as they tend to cook faster.

Remove from the hot oil and drain on paper towels. Serve on a warmed platter garnished with lemon wedges and fresh parsley sprigs.

SERVES 4 TO 6

HAPPY CLAMS

1 cup whole baby clams,
  drained

2 cups bread crumbs or
  crushed crackers

½ teaspoon savory powder

½ teaspoon garlic salt

¼ teaspoon cayenne

½ teaspoon onion powder

2 eggs, beaten

2 tablespoons warm beer

Oil for frying

Preheat oil in deep fryer to 375 degrees F.

If the clams are frozen, thaw and drain. If fresh, rinse and drain. If from a can, rinse and drain. Get the idea?

Measure the bread crumbs, savory powder, garlic salt, cayenne, and onion powder into a brown paper bag. Close the bag and shake vigorously to mix well.

In a medium bowl, whisk the eggs and beer until lightly frothy. Gently stir in the drained clams and let soak for 3 to 4 minutes. Remove 5 or 6 clams at a time with a slotted spoon and drop into the paper bag. Shake, rattle, and roll until the clams are covered with the bread crumb mixture. Remove clams from the bag to a bowl and refrigerate until all the clams have been coated. Refrigerate for 15 to 20 minutes to set.

With a frying basket or a slotted spoon, slip 5 or 6 clams at a time into the hot oil and fry until golden, about 30 seconds, so watch carefully! Drain on paper towels and serve immediately.

SERVES 4

FRED'S FRIED SMELT

1 cup milk

Dash of Louisiana hot
    sauce (or your favorite
    hot sauce)

1 cup flour

1 teaspoon oregano

1 teaspoon garlic powder

Salt and pepper to taste

1 pound fresh smelt, rinsed
    and dried

Lemon slices for garnish

Fresh parsley for garnish

Oil for frying

Preheat the oil in a deep fryer to 375 degrees F.

In a wide, flat bowl, combine the milk and hot sauce. Measure the flour, oregano, garlic powder, salt, and pepper into a brown paper bag. Close the bag and shake vigorously to mix well.

Dip the smelts into the milk 4 or 5 at a time, then toss into the bag and shake to cover the fish with the seasoned flour. Remove the coated fish to a plate. Repeat until all the fish have been coated.

Slide the fish into the hot oil, 5 or 6 at a time, and cook until they are golden brown, 4 to 5 minutes. Remove the smelt from the hot oil with a slotted spoon and drain on paper towels. Arrange on a platter with the lemon slices and parsley sprigs. Serve immediately.

SERVES 4

NO. 6

GETABLES

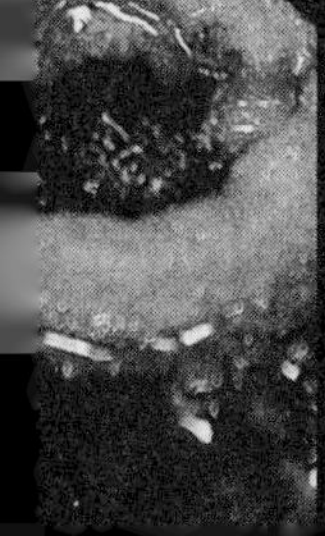

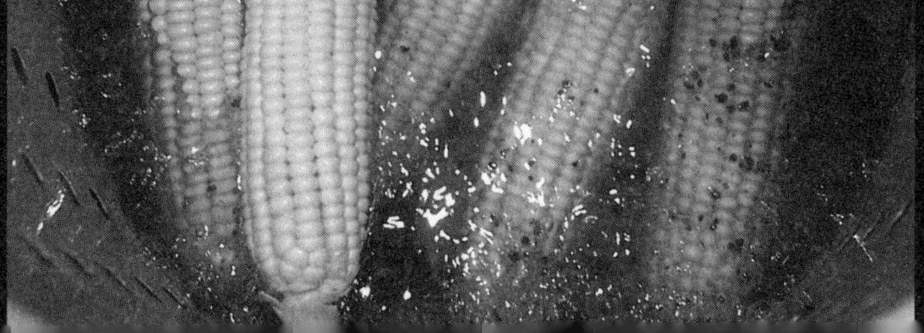

NO. 6

VEGETABLES

"BIG C" STUFFED PIEROGI

I GLEANED THIS RECIPE WHEN I VISITED CHICAGO ON SEVERAL COLLEGE WEEKENDS
AND ATE IN A POLISH NEIGHBORHOOD RESTAURANT. THE RESTAURANT HAS FADED FROM MY MEMORY,
BUT THE PIEROGI ARE FIRMLY IMPLANTED THERE, AND IN MY TUMMY AS WELL.

CHEESE/ONION/POTATO FILLING

½ cup chopped onion

2 tablespoons butter

½ teaspoon salt

¼ teaspoon dried chervil

¼ teaspoon dried sage

¼ teaspoon lemon pepper

2 cups mashed potatoes
   (instant varieties are okay)

1 cup grated sharp cheddar cheese

PIEROGI

2½ teaspoons salt

2 cups flour

2 eggs

⅓ cup water

Oil for frying

In a medium saucepan over medium heat, sauté the onions in the butter until they are soft, translucent, but not browned, about 5 minutes. Add the salt, chervil, sage, and pepper and stir.

Place the mashed potatoes in a large bowl and pour the onion-spice mixture over the potatoes. Add the grated cheese, and with a spoon blend well. Cover with plastic wrap and set the filling aside.

In a large pot on your stove, bring 4 to 5 inches of water to a boil. Add 2 teaspoons of salt.

To make the pierogi, place the flour in a large bowl and make a "well" in the center of the flour. Break the eggs into a small bowl, add the water and the remaining ½ teaspoon salt. Whisk the ingredients together, and then pour the liquid into the flour "well."

Mix the flour into the liquid in the center with one hand. Knead the dough until it's firm and well mixed. Cover the bowl of dough with a warm, moist towel and set it aside to rest for 10 to 15 minutes.

Cut the dough in half. Roll half of it out on a floured board to ⅛-inch thickness. Cover this with a moist towel and set aside. Repeat with the other half of the dough. Using a biscuit or cookie cutter, or wide drinking glass, cut 3-inch circles in the dough. Repeat rolling and cutting until all the dough has been used.

Place a small spoonful of filling a little to one side of the center of each dough circle. Moisten the edge with your fingertip dipped in water. Fold the circles in half and pinch the edges together to seal. Then, using a fork dipped in flour, seal the edges firmly to prevent the filling from leaking out during frying.

Heat the oil in a Dutch oven or deep pot fryer to 350 degrees F.

Slide 2 to 3 pierogi into the boiling salted water and cook for 3 to 5 minutes or until they float to the surface. Don't try to cook too many pierogi at the same time. They will stick together and cook unevenly.

With a slotted spoon or spatula remove the pierogi from the water and place them in a colander to drain. Make sure they are not touching one another or they will stick together. When well drained place them on a piece of foil. Boil up all the remaining dumplings.

With tongs or a spatula, slide the pierogi into the deep-frying oil, again 2 to 3 at a time, and cook until they are brown all over, 1 to 2 minutes. Remove them from the hot oil with a slotted spoon or spatula and serve very hot.

SERVES 4 TO 6

BAHAMIAN PLANTAINS

1 teaspoon sugar

1½ tablespoons sea salt

4 large green plantains

Oil for frying

Heat the oil in a deep fryer to 375 degrees F.

Mix the sugar and salt in small bowl and set aside.

Peel the plantains and cut them in 1-inch-thick slices at an angle so they are oval shaped. Place 8 to 10 plantain ovals in a deep frying basket so they are not touching, and fry them until they are slightly soft and their edges just start to brown. Remove them from the oil, drain, and cool on paper towels. Fry up the rest of the plantain ovals in the same fashion.

Place the plantains on a sheet of wax paper, cover them with another piece of wax paper, and gently use a rolling pin or thick glass to flatten the plantains to ½ inch thick.

Put plantains back into the oil and fry them 3 to 4 minutes, until golden. Using a large spatula or slotted spoon, remove them from the oil to some paper towels. Drain, season them with the salt and sugar mix, and serve warm.

SERVES 4 TO 6

BUGS BUNNY FRITTERS

10 carrots, cleaned and
   peeled

2 eggs

1 cup plus 3 tablespoons
   flour

2 tablespoons chopped
   peanuts

1 tablespoon brown sugar

1 tablespoon baking powder

1 tablespoon cornstarch

¼ teaspoon salt

White pepper to taste

Oil for frying

Heat oil in a Dutch oven or deep frying pot to 350 degrees F.

In a large saucepan over high heat, boil the carrots until tender, about 20 minutes. Place the carrots in a food processor and finely chop them.

In a large bowl, add the carrots, eggs, 3 tablespoons flour, chopped peanuts, sugar, baking powder, and cornstarch. Using the pulse button, blend the mixture for about 5 seconds, then season with salt and pepper.

Form the mixture into 3-inch oblong fritters and dust them in the remaining 1 cup flour. Let them firm for 5 minutes on a sheet of foil or wax paper.

Carefully slip the fritters into the hot oil and cook until they begin to brown and start to float, 3 to 4 minutes.

Remove with a slotted spoon or spatula, and drain on paper towels. Serve hot.

SERVES 4 TO 6

DOROTHY'S CORN-ON-THE-COB

6 ears of corn, shucked

12 tablespoons
confectioners' sugar

12 cups water

Oil for frying

Wash corn cobs. In a large pot add the sugar to the water and soak the corn in it for 1 to 2 hours. Drain and dry thoroughly.

Heat the oil in a deep fryer to 300 degrees F.

Fry all 6 corn cobs in the oil for 3 minutes. Do not allow any of the kernels to brown during the frying. Drain the corn well in a frying basket or on absorbent paper towels. If you use frozen corn, thaw before putting in the sugar water. Fry for 4 minutes instead of 3. Serve with melted butter.

SERVES 4 TO 6

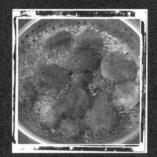

"FRYED" 'SHROOMS

BATTER

¾ cup water

1 cup self-rising flour

2 tablespoons vegetable oil

3 tablespoons chopped fresh
    parsley

MARINADE

¾ teaspoon onion salt

½ teaspoon Chinese five-spice
    powder

1 tablespoon minced fresh
    parsley

½ teaspoon powdered ginger

1 teaspoon rice wine

1 pound button or cremini
    mushrooms

2 tablespoons self-rising flour

¾ teaspoon seasoned salt

Pinch of citrus pepper

Parmesan cheese to sprinkle

Oil for frying

Heat the oil in a deep fryer to 375 degrees F.

Blend the water with 1 cup self-rising flour and stir until smooth. Let the batter stand for 5 to 10 minutes, and then add the vegetable oil and parsley. While the batter is resting, mix the marinade ingredients well in a small bowl.

Remove the stalks from the mushrooms and brush off any dirt. Blanch mushrooms for 1 minute in a large saucepan of boiling water, and then drain.

Place mushrooms in a wide bowl, pour in marinade and stir. Let mushrooms rest for 15 to 20 minutes.

In a paper bag, put drained mushrooms and 2 tablespoons flour, shake the bag until the mushrooms are coated. Remove them and dip them in batter using a toothpick stuck into the mushrooms. Gently slide them into the frying oil and cook until slightly brown and crispy, 2 to 3 minutes.

Remove mushrooms from oil with a slotted spoon and drain them quickly on paper towels. Arrange the mushrooms on a plate and season them with seasoned salt and citrus pepper. Sprinkle them with Parmesan cheese and serve hot.

SERVES 4 TO 6

INDONESIAN MARTABAK
Veggie Wrap

DOUGH

2 cups flour

3 tablespoons oil

¾ cup water

Pinch of salt

FILLING

½ cup oil

**4 cloves garlic, peeled and
sliced**

2 medium shallots, minced

**1 medium onion, halved and
sliced**

**2 tablespoons chopped fresh
Italian parsley**

1 tablespoon curry powder

5 eggs, beaten

**1 stalk green onion, finely
sliced**

Salt to taste

White pepper to taste

Oil for frying

In a large bowl prepare the dough by combining all the dough ingredients, mixing well, and then kneading the dough into an oily elastic consistency. Cover the dough with a moist towel and leave it at room temperature for 2 hours.

Divide the dough into 4 pieces and roll each piece into a ball. With oiled hands place each piece on an oiled or marble surface and pull dough into a large thin circle. Place finished dough circles on a plate, separated by wax paper and set aside, covered with moist towel.

While the dough is resting, make the filling. In a medium saucepan over medium-high heat, heat the oil and sauté the garlic and shallots for a few seconds. Add the sliced onion and parsley, and continue stir-frying for another 2 minutes. Add the curry powder, mix well, and cook another 3 minutes. Set the filling aside to cool.

When mixture reaches room temperature, add 4 eggs, the green onion, salt, and pepper, and mix filling ingredients well.

Heat 2 inches of oil in a large Dutch oven to 375 degrees F. Fill the center of each of the dough circles with ¼ of the mixture. Spread the filling on one side of the dough, brush the edges of the dough lightly with the remaining beaten egg to help seal. Fold in the sides and ends to completely enclose the filling.

Fry the wraps in the oil until golden brown on one side, 2 to 3 minutes, then turn wraps over and fry the other side. Cut the vegetable wraps into thirds and serve with curry sauce, chutney, or teriyaki sauce.

SERVES 4 TO 6

KATHLEEN'S CAULIFLOWERETTES

1 large cauliflower

4 cups water

1 teaspoon garlic salt

1 teaspoon onion powder

1 teaspoon paprika

Oil for frying

Heat oil in a Dutch oven or deep pot fryer to 375 degrees F.

Cut away the stems, remove the green leaves, and cut the florets off the cauliflower. Discard the thick core stem. Wash the florets under cold running water.

In a large pot, bring the water to a boil over high heat, and add the salt. Drop in the cauliflower florets and cook, uncovered, for 10 minutes, or until the pieces are tender but still slightly resistant to being pierced with a fork.

Remove the florets with a slotted spoon and drain them in a colander. Pat the cauliflower completely dry with paper towels, and slip them (8 to 10 pieces at a time) into the hot oil. Fry until golden brown on all sides, 3 to 5 minutes.

When they are cooked, use a slotted spoon to remove them and drain them on paper towels. Place them in a warm bowl, sprinkle with the onion powder and paprika, and serve.

SERVES 4 TO 6

MAMA SIS'S OKRA

2 pounds okra

½ cup self-rising cornmeal

2 tablespoons self-rising
   flour

1 teaspoon paprika

1 teaspoon dried thyme

1 teaspoon garlic powder

¼ teaspoon cayenne pepper

Dash of salt and pepper

Oil for frying

Heat oil in a deep fryer to 375 degrees F.

Wash and cut the okra into ¼-inch pieces. In a medium bowl, mix the cornmeal, flour, and seasonings and pour into a paper bag. Add the okra and shake the bag until all the pieces are covered with the flour mixture.

Slip the floured okra into the fryer and cook for 4 to 5 minutes, until the okra is browned and crisp on the outside.

Drain the okra on paper towels and serve hot.

SERVES 6 TO 8

PERSIAN PAKORA
Deep-fried Vegetables

BATTER

1 cup flour

½ cup plain yogurt

Pinch of baking powder

1 teaspoon granulated garlic

Salt to taste

½ teaspoon chili powder

2 medium sweet potatoes,
   thinly sliced

1 medium eggplant, thinly
   sliced

2 medium red onions, thinly
   sliced

2 fresh lemons, quartered,
   for garnish

Oil for frying

In a large bowl, combine the batter ingredients, and let the batter rest for 10 to 15 minutes.

Heat the oil in a deep fryer to 375 degrees F.

Dip the vegetables in the batter to coat evenly, drain, and gently lower them into the oil. Fry the vegetables until golden on both sides, 2 to 3 minutes per side. Remove the veggies with a slotted spoon or spatula and drain them on a paper towel.

Serve hot with fresh lemon to squeeze over vegetables.

SERVES 4

QUEBEC FRENCH FRIES

FOR SOME REASON THE PEOPLE OF QUEBEC, CANADA, MAKE "THE WORLD'S BEST FRIES." THEY ARE OFTEN SERVED IN PAPER CONTAINERS WITH TOOTHPICKS TO PICK UP THE FRIES, AND WITH MALT VINEGAR AND SALT TO SPRINKLE OVER THEM. *MERCI BEAUCOUP*, MADAME CHENEVERT. FOR A FUN CHANGE TRY USING A SPIRAL POTATO CUTTER TO CUT YOUR SPUDS INTO LONG SPIRALS OF POTATO TO FRY. AVAILABLE IN KITCHEN STORES, OR ON THE WEB, THESE CUTTERS RANGE IN PRICE FROM $2.99 FOR THE NORPRO HAND-OPERATED CUTTER TO $179 FOR NEMCO'S MANUAL CUTTER. ELECTRIC CUTTERS ARE ALSO AVAILABLE, BUT THEY RANGE FROM $210 TO $890. MAN, YOU GOTTA REALLY, REALLY LIKE FRIED POTATOES TO GO THAT ROUTE, UNLESS YOU HAVE A RESTAURANT. BUT IF YOU HAVE A RESTAURANT, WHAT ARE YOU DOING HERE?

Peel the potatoes, square off the ends and sides, cut into ⅜-inch-thick slices and then cut these into ⅜-inch sticks.

4 to 8 Idaho, Bintje, or Russett potatoes (1 to 2 medium-sized potatoes per serving)

12 cups cold water

12 tablespoons confectioners' sugar

Salt or seasoned salt for sprinkling

Oil for frying

Soak the potato sticks in a large bowl of plain water for 2 to 3 hours, to leach out the excess starch.

While the potatoes soak in the plain water, put the cold water in a deep bowl, add the confectioners' sugar, and stir until the sugar dissolves, 2 to 3 minutes.

Drain the potatoes and put them into the sugar-water, soaking them for 20 to 25 minutes.

Heat oil in a deep fryer or Dutch oven to 335 degrees F.

Take approximately one third of the potatoes and drain them (patting them dry with a paper towel is also a good idea), then place potatoes in a fryer basket. Only fill the basket about one third full as the potatoes need room to cook properly. Stir with a long spoon or long tongs after 30 seconds or so.

Preheat oven to 200 degrees F.

After about 2 to 3 minutes the potatoes should just be getting tender and will begin to turn a light brown. Remove the fries, transfer them to a wire rack, and cool. Fry up another batch. Repeat these steps until all the potatoes are cooked, drained, and cooled.

Make sure the fryer temperature is still at 335 degrees F.

Put potatoes back into fryer in same-sized batches as you did the first time, and fry each batch for 1 to 2 minutes. When the batches are finished, place them in the oven to keep warm, until all fries are cooked.

Serve potatoes immediately, sprinkled with salt or seasoned salt. Accompany with homemade mayonnaise, a 50/50 ketchup-mayonnaise mix, or top-quality malt vinegar.

SERVES 4

THE REAL FRIED GREEN TOMATOES

4 large firm underripe tomatoes

1 cup polenta or coarse
  cornmeal

1 teaspoon dried oregano

½ teaspoon garlic granules

1 cup flour

2 large eggs, beaten

Salt and pepper to taste

Oil for frying

Heat the oil in a Dutch oven or deep fryer to 375 degrees F.

Cut the tomatoes into 1-inch-thick slices and set aside. In a flat pan or dish, mix the polenta or cornmeal with the oregano and garlic. Place the flour, the eggs, and the polenta mixture in three separate bowls. Salt and pepper the slices to taste, coat them with the flour, dip the slices into the egg, and then cover both sides in the polenta.

Fry tomato slices in the hot oil on each side until crisp and golden brown, 2 to 3 minutes. Remove slices from oil with a slotted spoon, and drain over paper towels.

SERVES 4 TO 6

WALLA WALLA ONION RINGS

4 large Walla Walla, Vidalia,
  or other sweet onions

¾ cup flour

¼ cup cornstarch

1 teaspoon salt plus more to
  taste

1 teaspoon dried thyme

1 teaspoon dried summer
  savory

1 teaspoon onion powder

1 teaspoon paprika

1 teaspoon white pepper

1 teaspoon sugar

1 large egg, beaten

2 tablespoons vegetable oil

½ to ¾ cup dark beer

Oil for frying

On a cutting board, cut the onions into ½-inch-thick rings. Place the rings in cold water in a large bowl or pot and soak for 25 to 35 minutes. Drain the rings very well and pat very dry with paper towels.

In a large, flat bowl, mix the flour, cornstarch, salt, spices, and sugar. Then add the egg, vegetable oil, and beer, and mix gently with a large spoon until you get a thick batter. Let the batter rest at room temperature for 30 minutes.

Heat the oil in a deep fryer or Dutch oven to 375 degrees F. Preheat oven to 200 degrees F.

Dip the onion rings into the thick batter, draining off any excess, then place 4 to 5 of the rings in the hot oil. Do not overcrowd, as the rings need space to cook properly and might stick together if too many are cooked at the same time. Fry the rings for 2 to 3 minutes, until golden brown. Remove onions from oil with a slotted spoon or frying basket and keep them warm in the oven, on a paper-towel-covered platter. Season onion rings with salt or seasoned salt and serve very hot.

SERVES 4 TO 6

WHITE CORN AND SWEET PEPPER FRITTERS

1 tablespoon extra-virgin olive oil

½ cup chopped sweet onion

¼ cup finely chopped red bell peppers

¼ cup finely chopped yellow bell
  peppers

2 cups white corn kernels, about 4
  medium ears

2 tablespoons minced garlic

Salt and pepper to taste

¼ cup minced green onions

3 eggs, beaten

1½ cups milk

1¼ cups cornmeal

2 cups flour

1 tablespoon brown sugar

1 teaspoon paprika

1 teaspoon dried basil

1 teaspoon cayenne pepper

2 teaspoons baking powder

Dash of hot sauce

Oil for frying

Heat the oil in a Dutch oven to 375 degrees F.

Heat the olive oil in a nonstick pan and add the onion, peppers, corn, and garlic. Season with salt and pepper, and cook for about 2 minutes. Add in the green onions, stir, remove pan from the heat, and set it aside to cool.

In a separate bowl, beat the eggs and milk together and season with salt and pepper. Add the cornmeal, flour, brown sugar, paprika, basil, cayenne, and baking powder, whisking mixture until the batter is smooth and free of lumps.

Pour the corn mixture into the batter, season it with a dash of hot sauce, and let the mixture rest for 10 minutes.

Using a large serving spoon, drop a heaping spoonful at a time into hot oil. When the fritters pop to the surface, use a slotted spoon to turn them over so they brown evenly on both sides. Fry 4 to 5 minutes, until golden brown.

Remove fritters from the oil with a slotted spoon and drain them on paper towels. Serve hot.

SERVES 6 TO 8

PARISIAN FRIED SWEET TATERS

1 tablespoon granulated
  sugar

1 teaspoon salt

1 teaspoon pepper

1 teaspoon onion powder

Pinch of dry mustard

2 medium sweet potatoes
  (about 2 pounds)

Oil for frying

Preheat the frying oil in a deep fryer to 400 degrees F.

In a medium bowl, combine the sugar, salt, pepper, onion powder, and mustard, and stir well. Set aside.

Wash and peel the potatoes. Cut lengthwise into ½-by-½-inch strips. Pat the strips dry with paper towels and set them aside.

Fry 3 or 4 strips at a time in the hot oil, for 3 to 3½ minutes, or until golden brown. Remove from the oil with a slotted spoon and immediately roll the strips in the sugar-spice mixture. Repeat until all the strips have been cooked and rolled in the mixture. Serve immediately.

SERVES 6

'SMARVELOUS 'SPARAGUS

1 teaspoon salt

½ teaspoon white pepper

Pinch of lemon granules

1 pound fresh asparagus
   stalks, bottom 1 to 2
   inches trimmed and
   patted dry

2 tablespoons fresh
   lemon juice

Oil for frying

Preheat the oil in a deep fryer to 370 degrees F.

In a small bowl or shaker mix the salt, pepper, and lemon granules. Set aside.

Slip 4 or 5 asparagus stalks into the hot oil at a time. Fry until they begin to brown, about 5 minutes. Remove from the hot oil with a slotted spoon or spatula and drain on paper towels. Sprinkle the stalks with the salt mixture.

Repeat until all the stalks are cooked and sprinkled. Place on a very hot platter and drizzle with the fresh lemon juice just before serving.

SERVES 4

PARMESAN EGGPLANT ROUNDS

1 large eggplant (about 1 to 1½ pounds), peeled and cut into ¾-inch slices

1 tablespoon salt or less, depending on volume of eggplant

BREADING

½ cup flour

¾ cup cornmeal

½ teaspoon garlic powder

1 teaspoon onion powder

1 teaspoon salt

1 teaspoon citrus (or lemon) pepper

½ cup freshly grated Parmigiano-Reggiano

Oil for frying

Preheat the oil in a deep fryer to 375 degrees F.

Sprinkle the eggplant slices liberally with salt and let them stand on paper towels for 30 minutes (this draws out the bitterness of the eggplant). Rinse the eggplant to remove any remaining salt and pat the slices dry.

Combine the breading ingredients in a wide, shallow bowl and stir well. Dredge the eggplant slices in the mixture and slip each slice carefully into the hot oil. Do not try to cook more than 3 or 4 slices at a time. Fry until golden brown, 2 to 3 minutes.

Remove the slices from the oil with a slotted spoon and drain them on paper towels. Sprinkle with the Parmigiano-Reggiano (the Mercedes-Benz of Parmesan cheeses) and serve very hot.

SERVES 6

MAMSELLE'S CRISPY OKRA

1½ pounds fresh okra

2 eggs, beaten

¼ cup beer

4 tablespoons Louisiana hot
  sauce (or other favorite
  hot sauce)

¼ cup flour

1 cup white or yellow
  cornmeal

1 teaspoon salt

1 teaspoon garlic powder

1 teaspoon white pepper

Oil for frying

Preheat the oil in a deep fryer to 375 degrees F.

Wash the okra, making sure to get all the sand off the stalks. Cut into ½-inch slices.

In a wide, shallow bowl combine the eggs, beer, and hot sauce and whisk until well blended. In a second shallow, flat bowl mix together the flour, cornmeal, salt, garlic powder, and pepper and stir well. Thoroughly coat the okra slices in the egg mixture, then dredge them well in the cornmeal mixture.

Slip the okra slices into the hot oil in small batches, and cook until they are golden brown, 4 to 5 minutes.

Remove the okra slices from the hot oil with a slotted spoon and drain them briefly on paper towels. Serve the okra hot with chilled adult beverages, preferably those made with hops and malt.

SERVES 4 TO 6

ELMER'S B'WEADED B'WOCCOLI

1 large head of broccoli
   (about 2 pounds)
2 eggs, beaten
3 tablespoons white wine
Salt and pepper to taste
1 cup flour
2 cups seasoned bread
   crumbs
1 tablespoon onion flakes
1 teaspoon paprika

Oil for frying

Preheat oil for deep frying to 375 degrees F.

Clean and cut the broccoli stalks into florets, leaving the stems attached. Place the broccoli in a large pot and cover with salted water. Bring to a boil over high heat, then lower the heat to medium and boil rapidly for 4 to 5 minutes.

Drain the broccoli in a colander and plunge it into an ice water bath to keep the color a bright green. Drain the florets thoroughly and pat dry.

In a shallow bowl, combine the eggs, wine, and salt and pepper and whisk until well mixed. In a separate shallow bowl, mix the flour, bread crumbs, onion flakes, and paprika.

Dip the broccoli stalks into the egg mixture, then dredge them in the bread crumb mixture until well coated. Slip the breaded vegetables into the hot oil with a slotted spoon, 4 or 5 pieces at a time. Fry the broccoli until golden brown, 3 or 4 minutes.

Remove the broccoli from the hot oil with a slotted spoon and drain it on paper towels. Serve on a heated platter.

SERVES 6 TO 8

NO. 7

DESSERTS

NO. 7

DESSERTS

BLACK FOREST APPLE FRITTERS

1½ cups flour

¼ teaspoon salt

3 eggs

1 cup hard apple cider

4 Pippin, Granny Smith, or
    Golden Delicious apples

½ cup confectioners' sugar

1 teaspoon ground cinnamon

1 teaspoon ground nutmeg

¼ teaspoon ground allspice

Dash of ground cloves

Oil for frying

Place the flour and salt in a large mixing bowl. Add the eggs and slowly stir in the cider to make a thick batter. Let the batter rest for 10 minutes.

Heat the oil in a deep fryer or Dutch oven to 350 degrees F.

Peel, core, and cut the apples into 1-inch slices. Pat the apple slices dry with a paper towel, dip the slices in the batter, and then deep-fry them until golden brown, 2 to 2½ minutes. Drain on paper towels.

Mix the confectioners' sugar, cinnamon, nutmeg, allspice, and cloves and put the mix in a sifter or shaker with large holes.

Serve the apple fritters warm, sprinkled with the sugar and spice mixture.

SERVES 4 TO 8

CAMEMBERT AND BRIE WITH PEARS (OR APPLES)

USE BOSC OR COMICE PEARS OR EVEN PIPPIN OR GRANNY SMITH APPLES. BETTER YET, USE SOME OF EACH. DO NOT USE DRIED OR COMMERCIALLY PACKAGED BREAD CRUMBS, USE ONLY FRESH CRUMBS THAT YOU MAKE YOURSELF.

½ pound Camembert

½ pound Brie

4 slices fresh white
  bread, crusts removed

2 eggs

2 tablespoons water

6 pears or apples

2 teaspoons freshly
  squeezed lemon juice

Oil for frying

Slice the cheeses into 12 wedges each and chill them in a refrigerator for 30 minutes. Place the bread slices in a food processor and pulse until you get very fine crumbs. Place the crumbs in a shallow dish. In a small bowl, whisk the eggs, add the water, and whisk again.

Dip the chilled cheese wedges into the egg mixture and then roll the wedges in the bread crumbs. Then dip the cheese wedges again into the egg mixture, and roll in bread crumbs once more.

Place the crumbed cheese wedges on a sheet of aluminum foil and chill them for 1 to 2 hours. Just before cooking the cheese, slice and remove the cores of the pears (and/or apples) and sprinkle them with lemon juice to prevent the fruit from turning brown.

Heat oil in a deep fryer to 375 degrees F.

Carefully place the breaded cheese wedges into hot oil for about 2 minutes or until the crumbs are golden brown. Remove with a spatula or slotted spoon and drain on paper towels. Cool slightly.

Serve warm on a platter with sliced fruit.

SERVES 8 TO 10

CITRUS-Y CHURROS

Fresh strips of zest from
  3 lemons and 3 limes
½ cup hot water
1 stick butter, cut in 4 pieces
2 tablespoons white sugar
1 cup flour
4 eggs, beaten
1 tablespoon granulated
  orange zest
1 tablespoon white or brown
  sugar
1 tablespoon ground
  cinnamon
½ teaspoon ground nutmeg

Oil for frying

Heat the oil in a deep fryer to 375 degrees F. As it is heating, add the lemon and lime zest to the oil. When you reach the proper temperature, remove the fried zests with a slotted spoon and discard.

In a medium saucepan over medium heat, combine the water, butter, 2 tablespoons white sugar, and the flour and stir rapidly with a wooden spoon until the mixture forms a ball that pulls away from the sides of the pan.

Take pan off the heat and beat in the eggs and orange zest. Spoon the dough into a pastry bag equipped with a large star tip (#6) and pipe 5- to 6-inch-long ribbons of dough directly into the hot oil, cutting dough off with a sharp knife.

For the best results fry only a couple of churros at a time. Cook them until golden brown, approximately 2½ minutes, then drain the pastry on a wire cake rack placed over paper towels.

In a small bowl or saucer, mix together 1 tablespoon white or brown sugar, cinnamon, and nutmeg. Put mixture in a sifter and sift the spices over the hot churros, turning to coat both sides of the pastries. Serve hot.

SERVES 8 TO 10

FRIED AND CARAMELIZED APPLES

BATTER

½ cup flour

2 tablespoons cornstarch

¾ teaspoon baking powder

½ cup beer

2 Golden Delicious or Gala
apples

SYRUP

⅔ cup sugar

⅓ cup warm water

1 tablespoon salad oil

Oil for frying

Nonstick cooking spray

Heat oil in a Dutch oven or deep pot fryer to 350 degrees F.

To make the batter, mix the flour, cornstarch, and baking powder in a medium bowl. Add the beer and stir until smooth.

Peel and core the apples. Cut each apple into 4 wedges. Drop the apples into the bowl of batter and turn to coat evenly.

Lift one piece of fruit at a time from the bowl and let the excess batter drip off. Gently lower the apple wedges into the hot oil. Cook several pieces at a time until the coating is golden brown, about 2 minutes. Remove the wedges with a slotted spoon and drain them on paper towels.

Fill a large serving bowl to the brim with ice cubes and cover the ice with water. Spray a dish with cooking spray and set aside.

Combine the sugar, water, and salad oil in a medium frying pan and stir to blend. Place the pan over high heat. When the mixture begins to bubble, about 1 minute, shake the pan continuously to prevent the liquid from burning.

Continue cooking and shaking the pan until the syrup barely begins to turn a pale straw color, 8 to 9 minutes. Immediately remove the pan from the heat. The syrup will continue to cook and it will turn golden in a few seconds.

Carefully slide the fried apples into the syrup, 2 to 3 at a time, and swirl the pan to coat the wedges evenly. Using two spoons, immediately remove each piece of fruit and place on the oiled dish, making sure that the pieces do not touch.

When still hot to the touch, quickly dip each piece of fruit into the ice water so the sugar coating hardens and the fruit cools enough to eat. Serve immediately thereafter.

SERVES 6

FRIED CUSTARD SQUARES WITH LEMON-RASPBERRY SAUCE

CUSTARD

2 cups milk

1 cinnamon stick

1 (3- to 4-inch-long) piece lemon zest

6 egg yolks

⅓ cup cornstarch

½ cup granulated sugar

½ teaspoon salt

BREADING

1 cup fine dry bread crumbs

¼ cup granulated sugar

1½ teaspoons ground cinnamon

2 eggs, lightly beaten

1 cup flour

SAUCE

1½ cups water

1 cup firmly packed light brown sugar

½ cup plus 1 tablespoon light rum

Fresh lemon juice to taste

Fresh golden raspberries for garnish

Oil for frying

Butter an 8-inch square baking pan. In a heavy saucepan bring the milk just to a boil with the cinnamon stick and the lemon zest floating on the surface. Keep at a bare simmer for 15 minutes. Discard the cinnamon stick and zest, then pour the hot milk through a fine sieve into a 4-cup glass measuring cup.

In a bowl, beat the egg yolks, cornstarch, sugar, and salt together. While slowly pouring in the milk, whisk the mixture until smooth. Pour the resulting custard into the milk saucepan, whisking continually, and bring it to a boil over high heat. Let it boil for 1 minute while whisking with vigor, then take it off the heat. The custard now should be smooth and thickened, and give off a nice cinnamon and lemon scent.

Immediately pour the custard into the prepared baking pan, smoothing the top and covering it with a piece of buttered wax paper in which you've punched some small holes (to let any steam escape). Chill the custard in a refrigerator until firm, 1½ to 2 hours. Then with a knife dipped in hot water, cut the custard into 2-inch squares.

For the breading: in a small bowl mix the bread crumbs, sugar, and ground cinnamon. In a shallow dish lightly whisk the eggs. Working with 1 custard square at a time, coat the custard squares with flour, shaking off the excess, and then dip them into the eggs, letting the excess drip off into the bowl. Gently coat the custards with the bread crumb mixture on all sides. Then transfer the coated pieces to a wax-paper-lined cookie sheet. Chill squares, uncovered, for 30 minutes.

For the sauce: in a medium saucepan, combine the water, sugar, and ½ cup rum, and simmer, uncovered, for 15 to 18 minutes. Stir in the remaining 1 tablespoon of rum and the lemon juice and pour the mixture into a small bowl.

Heat 3 inches of oil in a deep frying pot or a heavy Dutch oven to 375 degrees F. Place a cake rack in an oven set to 200 degrees F.

Fry 2 to 3 squares until they are golden, 15 to 20 seconds per side. Dip the blade of a spatula in hot oil (to prevent custards from sticking), carefully lift the fried squares out of the oil with the spatula, and place the custard squares on the cake rack in the oven to drain and keep warm.

Pour a generous amount (2 to 3 tablespoons) of sauce onto 8 dessert plates. Place 2 custard squares on each plate and garnish with golden raspberries.

SERVES 8

FRIED ICE CREAM— NO KIDDING!

1 pint top quality vanilla ice cream

3 eggs, beaten

1 teaspoon vanilla

1 cup finely crushed vanilla wafers

3 cups finely crushed honey-nut cornflakes

1 teaspoon ground cinnamon

OPTIONAL GARNISH

Whipped cream

Chocolate syrup

Rainbow-colored sprinkles

Maraschino cherries

Oil for frying

Divide the ice cream into 4 equal portions. Wearing rubber gloves, which you may keep dipping into a bowl of hot water, form the ice cream portions into 4 equal-sized balls. Place them side by side, but not touching, on a freezer-safe plate, and freeze them until firm, at least 1 hour.

In a small bowl, beat the eggs and vanilla together. In a wide, flat bowl, mix together the vanilla wafers, cornflakes, and cinnamon.

Remove the ice cream balls from the freezer. Roll each ball in the egg mixture and then roll them in the cereal mixture. Return the ice cream to the freezer.

After 1 hour remove the balls from the freezer and repeat the dipping and rolling process for a second time. Make sure the ice cream is evenly covered with crumbs. If you wish, you may dip and reroll the balls in the dry mix a third time, but usually twice is enough to obtain a good coating.

Return the ice cream balls to the freezer and leave for 3 to 4 hours, or ideally, overnight, until they are frozen solid.

Heat at least 3 inches of oil in a deep fryer or large Dutch oven to 375 degrees F. With a large slotted spoon, slip the ice cream into the hot oil, and fry the ice cream balls 1 at a time for 15 to 20 seconds or until the crumbs are golden brown. Do not try to do all four ice cream balls at once, as the last one you remove may already be melting inside.

Remove the ice cream balls from the oil and drain on paper towels, in a chilled dish. Serve immediately.

Garnish with whipped cream, chocolate syrup, rainbow-colored sprinkles, and maraschino cherries as desired.

SERVES 4

HUNGARIAN CHERRIES (OR PLUMS)

1 pound fresh ripe red cherries, stems
    on (or 1- to 1½-inch plums)

3 eggs

⅓ cup dry white wine

¼ cup sugar

⅓ cup milk

1 cup flour

Confectioners' sugar for sprinkling

Ground cinnamon or nutmeg for
    sprinkling

Oil for frying

Heat the oil in a deep fryer to 375 degrees F.

Wash the cherries and wipe them dry. *Do not remove their stems.* Tie the stems together with thread to form clusters of 3 or 4.

Combine the eggs, white wine, sugar, milk, and flour in a medium bowl and mix well to make a smooth batter.

Dip each cherry cluster into the thick batter, coating the cherries completely. Carefully lower cherry clusters into the hot oil. When cherries are golden, in 2 to 3 minutes, remove them with a slotted spoon and drain on paper towels.

Sprinkle with confectioners' sugar and a tiny bit of cinnamon (or nutmeg) on each cluster and serve warm.

SERVES 6

MAUDIE FRICKERT'S FRIED CHEESECAKE

CHEESECAKE? FRIED? YOU GOTTA BE KIDDING! BUT NO, I'M NOT! YOU WON'T BELIEVE HOW DELICIOUS THIS RECIPE IS. PLUS, IT'S WORTH THE EFFORT TO WATCH YOUR GUESTS' REACTION WHEN THEY CUT INTO A SPRING ROLL WRAPPER TO DISCOVER A TASTY DESSERT.

TOPPING MIXTURE

1 cup confectioners' sugar

½ cup Nestle's chocolate drink powder

1 medium to large cheesecake, thawed

1 cup milk (or light cream)

1 egg

30 spring roll wrappers

Oil for frying

Heat the oil in a Dutch oven or deep frying pot to 365 degrees F.

Mix the sugar and chocolate drink powder in flat bowl or pan, and set it aside.

Cut the cheesecake into 1- × 3-inch pieces. Beat the milk (or cream) and egg in a small bowl. Lightly moisten each spring roll wrapper with this mixture.

Place a piece of cheesecake in the center of a moistened wrapper. Fold the top of each wrapper down over the cheesecake pieces, and then fold both sides toward the middle. Roll each piece of cheesecake toward you until it is completely rolled up. Gently squeeze the cheesecake rolls to make sure the dough is sealed completely. Repeat until all cheesecake and/or spring roll wrappers are used.

Slip 2 to 3 rolls at a time into the hot oil, and allow them to brown lightly, 10 to 15 seconds. Using tongs or a spatula, remove the browned rolls from the oil. Place each roll in the bowl of sugar–chocolate powder and turn over to coat well.

Place the deep-fried cheesecake rolls on paper towels to cool slightly before serving, about 5 minutes, as the inside will be very hot. Best served immediately after they've cooled, on a warm dessert plate, but these can also be eaten cold.

SERVES 8 TO 10

MOMMA'S ZEPPOLES

Italian Dessert Pastries

2 cups hot water

1 cup butter

2 cups flour

1¼ cups granulated sugar

4 egg yolks

Pinch of salt

¼ cup marsala wine

1 teaspoon vanilla extract

1 cup cold water

Confectioners' sugar for sprinkling

Granulated sugar and cinnamon for sprinkling

Melted honey for drizzling

Oil for frying

In a medium pot over high heat, heat the hot water and butter until boiling. Add the flour, and stir over the heat until the mixture dries and begins to pull away from the pan, 2 to 5 minutes.

Remove the pan from the heat, and then slowly add the granulated sugar, egg yolks, salt, wine, and vanilla, mixing them well. Form into a dough, and lightly knead for 5 minutes or so until the dough is satiny. Cover it with plastic wrap, or a moist towel, and let it sit at room temperature for 30 minutes.

Heat the oil in a deep fryer to 350 degrees F.

Divide the dough into 3 parts. Take 1 part and break off small pieces from it that you can roll into a thickness about the width of your finger, by 8 inches long. Join the ends in a circle like a thin doughnut, moistening both ends with cold water so they'll stick together.

Fry in oil until they become golden brown, 3 to 4 minutes. Drain on a plate covered with paper towels, and lightly dust with confectioners' sugar or the sugar and cinnamon mix, or brush with melted honey.

SERVES 6 TO 8

PEACH AND APRICOT FRY-PIES

PASTRY

4 cups flour

1 teaspoon salt

1 cup lard

1 cup milk

FILLING

8 ounces dried apricots

6 ounces dried peaches

1 teaspoon vanilla

¾ cup firmly packed brown sugar

4 tablespoons butter

1 egg

1 tablespoon milk

Confectioners' sugar for sprinkling

Vegetable oil for frying

In a large bowl, mix together the flour and salt. Using a fork or a pastry blender cut in the lard until the mixture is crumbly. Mix in the milk, and stir until the dough forms a ball. Cover and refrigerate the dough for 1 hour.

Remove dough from refrigerator and, using a floured cutting board, roll out the dough and cut it into 16 (6-inch) circles. Set aside.

In a large saucepan, combine the apricots, peaches, vanilla, and sugar. Add enough water to cover the fruit. Cover the pan and cook over low heat until the fruit is falling apart, 25 to 30 minutes. Remove the lid and continue to cook until all of the water is evaporated. Take the pan off the heat and with a spoon stir in the butter.

Heat the oil in a deep fryer to 350 degrees F.

Spoon equal amounts of the filling onto one half of each pastry circle and fold the circle in half. Beat the egg with the milk. Brush egg-milk mixture on the bottom edge of the pastry and seal it with a fork dipped in cold water.

Place in frying basket and slowly lower into the oil. Fry 1 to 2 pies at a time in the hot oil, browning them on both sides, 2 to 3 minutes. Remove pies from the hot oil and drain the pies on paper towels.

While the pastry is still hot, sprinkle with confectioners' sugar.

SERVES 10 TO 12

SONGKRAN BANANA FRITTERS

6 small half-ripe bananas

Lemon juice

BATTER

½ cup flour

2 tablespoons cornstarch

¼ cup granulated sugar

¼ teaspoon salt

½ cup water

1 teaspoon banana liqueur

½ cup shredded coconut

Confectioners' sugar and
    cardamom for sprinkling

Canola oil for frying

Peel the bananas and cut them crosswise into 3- to 4-inch lengths. Brush them with lemon juice so they won't turn brown, and set aside.

In a medium bowl, sift together the flour, cornstarch, sugar, and salt. Add the water slowly while stirring constantly with a large spoon. Add liqueur, then continue to stir until the batter is smooth and thick enough to lightly coat the back of a spoon. Add the coconut and gently fold into the batter.

Heat 3 inches of oil in a deep fryer or Dutch oven to 375 degrees F. Preheat oven to 200 degrees F.

Slide the bananas into the batter. Using a long bamboo or metal skewer, lift out the coated banana pieces one at a time, allowing the excess batter to drop into the bowl. Carefully lower each piece of banana into the hot oil. Do not fry more than 3 to 4 pieces at a time as the fruit must be able to float freely.

Deep-fry, turning often with chopsticks or slotted spoon, until golden brown, 2 to 2½ minutes. Drain fried bananas on paper towels, and place on a platter in the oven to keep warm. Repeat with the remaining pieces of banana.

Arrange the bananas on a lettuce leaf, on a warmed platter, and sprinkle them using a shaker of confectioners' sugar to which you've added a pinch or two of cardamom.

SERVES 6

RB'S KEY LIME CRULLERS

Vegetable oil for foil

1 cup water

¼ cup lard

2 tablespoons granulated
    sugar

½ teaspoon salt

1¼ cups flour

4 eggs

1 tablespoon grated lime
    zest

LIME GLAZE

3 cups confectioners' sugar

1 teaspoon grated lime zest

4 tablespoons lime juice

Confectioners' sugar in sifter

Powdered lime granules
    (See Note)

Oil for frying

With scissors, cut 12 (4-inch) squares of aluminum foil, and generously brush one side of each square with vegetable oil. Using a 2 ½-inch round cookie cutter, score the center of each foil sheet for a guide to shape the crullers. Put foil on baking sheets.

In a large saucepan, combine the water, lard, sugar, and salt and bring to a full rolling boil over high heat. Quickly add the flour and beat vigorously with a wooden spoon until the dough forms a ball and pulls away from the pan. Remove the pan from heat.

Make a well in the center of the dough and add the eggs, beating with a wooden spoon after each egg is added, until the pastry is mixed, and is smooth and satin-like. Add the lime zest and mix well into the dough with a spoon.

Put the warm dough in large pastry bag. With a ½-inch large star-tip in place, squeeze the dough into circles onto the oiled and scored foil, using the circular marks on the foil to make circles of dough. Let the dough circles cool in the refrigerator for 15 to 20 minutes.

Heat the oil in a deep fryer to 375 degrees F.

Slide the dough circles off the foil into hot oil. Fry the crullers for 4 to 5 minutes, turning them several times, until both sides are brown and crullers puff up.

Remove crullers with a wire net or slotted spatula, and drain them on paper towels.

Mix the glaze ingredients together in a shallow, wide bowl. Let crullers cool for 5 minutes, then dip them halfway into glaze, and then let excess glaze drip back into the bowl. Place crullers glazed side up on a wire rack until the glaze sets. Sprinkle with confectioners' sugar and some of the powdered lime granules.

Serve crullers warm, with strong coffee.

Note: Lime granules are available on-line from www.oregonspice.com.

SERVES 6 TO 8

PETITE PEACH PIES

PASTRY

3 cups flour

1 teaspoon salt

¾ cup shortening or lard

1 large egg, beaten

¼ cup water

1 teaspoon apple cider
  vinegar

FILLING

4 cups chopped fresh
  peaches

1 cup water

1 cup peach wine

½ cup sugar

½ teaspoon ground nutmeg

Pinch of ground cloves

Sugar for sprinkling

Oil for frying

To make the pastry, mix the flour and salt in a large bowl. Cut in the shortening with a pastry blender and blend until the mixture resembles coarse meal. Combine the egg and water and sprinkle over the flour mixture. Add the vinegar, and stir with a fork, until the dry ingredients are moistened. Shape the mixture into a ball and wrap it in wax paper to chill in the refrigerator for at least 1 hour.

Divide the pastry into thirds. On a floured board, roll each portion to a ¼-inch thickness. Cut dough into 5-inch circles.

In a large saucepan, combine the peaches, water, and wine and bring to a boil over high heat. Reduce the heat, cover the saucepan, and simmer until tender, about 20 minutes.

Heat the oil in a Dutch oven or deep frying pot to 375 degrees F.

Cool the peaches and mash them slightly with a potato masher or large spoon. Stir in the sugar, nutmeg, and cloves.

Place about 2 tablespoons of the peach mixture on half of each pastry circle. To seal the pies, dip your fingers in cold water and moisten the edges of the pastry circles. Fold the circles in half, making sure the edges are even. Press the edges of the filled pastries firmly together using a fork dipped in flour.

When all the pies are made, slip 1 or 2 at a time into the hot oil. Fry the pies until they are golden brown on both sides, 4 to 5 minutes, turning once.

Drain the pies well on paper towels. Sprinkle them with sugar while the pies are still very warm, and serve.

SERVES 6 TO 12

GRANNY'S RAISIN-APPLE PIES

LARD IS THE BEST SHORTENING TO USE IN MAKING THE PASTRY CRUST,
BUT CRISCO OR OTHER SHORTENINGS WILL ALSO WORK.

PASTRY

2 cups flour

1 teaspoon salt

½ cup shortening

½ cup very cold water

FILLING

½ cup raisins (golden are nice)

1½ cups chopped apples
    (Pippins are nice)

½ cup water (or for a pie with
    more punch, ¼ cup water
    and ¼ cup apple brandy)

½ cup brown sugar, packed

½ teaspoon cinnamon

½ teaspoon nutmeg

⅛ teaspoon ground cloves

Confectioners' sugar for
    sprinkling

Oil for frying

Preheat the oil in a deep fryer to 365 degrees F.

To make the pastry, in a large bowl, combine the flour and salt. Using two forks, cut in the shortening until the mixture forms cornflake-size chunks. Sprinkle the cold water over the dough and mix it in lightly with the forks. Do not stir the dough or it will become hard and unworkable. Gently form the dough into a ball with your hands.

Divide the dough in half. Using a floured rolling pin, on a floured cutting board, roll out half of the dough to a ⅟₁₆-inch thickness. Using a small bowl or large cookie cutter, cut 5 circles (approximately 5 inches each in diameter) from the dough. Put the circles on a plate and chill them in the refrigerator while you repeat this process with the other half of the dough. Refrigerate the dough for 20 minutes.

In a large saucepan over high heat, combine the raisins, apples, and water and bring to a boil. Reduce the heat to low and cook for 5 minutes, stirring often. Add the brown sugar, cinnamon, nutmeg, and ground cloves and simmer for 5 minutes, again stirring frequently. Remove the pan from the heat and let the mixture cool.

Remove the dough from the refrigerator and place 2 tablespoons of apple filling in the center of each dough round. Using a pastry brush, wet the edges of the dough with cold water. Fold the filled circles of dough to make a half-moon shape and seal them with your fingers. Crimp the edges with the tines of a fork.

Slip 2 or 3 pies at a time into the hot oil and fry until golden, 3 to 4 minutes. Remove the pies from the hot oil and drain on paper towels. Sprinkle liberally with confectioners' sugar just before serving.

SERVES 10

PRAMOD'S GULAB JAMUNS

GULAB JAMUNS, A DESSERT FAVORITE IN INDIA, ARE ROUND, SUGARY PANCAKE BALLS COVERED IN A THICK, ROSE-SCENTED SUGAR SYRUP. THIS RECIPE IS DEDICATED TO PRAMOD PARIKH, A GENTLE, RELIGIOUS MAN WHO HAPPENED TO BE THE LOVING FATHER OF A CLOSE FRIEND OF MINE.

2½ cups powdered milk (such as
    Carnation or Nestlé)
½ cup flour
Pinch of baking soda
½ pint heavy whipping cream

SYRUP

3 cups sugar
5½ cups of water
1 teaspoon ground cardamom
1 tablespoon rose water or
    ½ teaspoon rose essence (not
    vital, but important if you
    want to taste the real thing)

Oil for frying

Preheat the oil in a deep fryer to *215 degrees F.* (This is a lower temperature than we're used to using in a deep fryer, but it's important for these delicate doughnut hole–like desserts.)

In a large bowl, combine the powdered milk, flour, and baking soda. Add the whipping cream and knead well until the dough is soft, moist, and pliant, 3 to 4 minutes. Set aside.

To make the syrup, in a large saucepan over high heat, combine the sugar and water and stir occasionally until boiling. Reduce the heat to medium-high and let it slowly boil for 4 to 6 minutes more. The syrup will thicken slightly and will lightly coat the back of a spoon. You do *not* want thick syrup as it will not be absorbed into the doughballs. Add the cardamom and stir, then turn the burner to its lowest setting to keep the syrup warm. Add the rose water and stir.

Take a pinch of the dough and roll it in your hands into ½-inch balls (*jamuns*). When all the dough has been used, slip 10 to 15 jamuns at a time into the hot oil, where they will sink to the bottom of the fryer. Using a long spoon, gently move the balls once or twice to keep them from browning on just one side.

After about 5 minutes, the balls will rise to the surface. Now they must be gently and constantly agitated with a wooden spoon to ensure even browning. Continue cooking until they are golden brown and floating on the surface, about 20 minutes.

Remove one ball and slip it into the syrup. If it doesn't collapse within 3 minutes, add the remaining balls. Otherwise, fry the balls for about 5 minutes more, then add them to the syrup. While the jamuns are in the syrup, squish each one lightly so that the syrup is more readily absorbed, but don't break them open. The balls should soak in the syrup for at least 2 hours before serving and may be stored, well-sealed and refrigerated, for up to 4 days. Return to room temperature or warm before serving.

MAKES 40 TO 50 GULAB JAMUNS

DEEP-FRIED TWINKIES

2 packages of Twinkies (4 cakes)

BATTER

2 cups flour

2 tablespoons cider or malt
   vinegar

2 teaspoons baking powder

1 teaspoon salt

¾ cup water

¾ cup beer

1 cup flour, for rolling

Fruit Sauce (recipe follows)

Confectioners' sugar, for
   sprinkling

Oil for frying

Unwrap the Twinkies. Push 1 Popsicle stick into one end of each cake until there is about 2 inches of stick left (this will make them easier to handle during following steps). Place the Twinkies on a plate, cover with plastic wrap, and freeze overnight.

The next day, heat the oil in a deep fryer to 350 degrees F.

In a large, flat bowl, mix the flour, vinegar, baking powder, salt, water, and beer together with a hand whisk until completely blended and smooth like a custard.

Remove the Twinkies from the freezer. Roll them in 1 cup of flour in a shallow pan or bowl, until they are well covered with the flour. Take the floured cakes and, holding on to the Popsicle sticks, dip each cake into batter. Coat each Twinkie well.

Slip the battered Twinkies into the deep fryer for 1 to 1½ minutes, or until the outside turns a nice golden brown. You'll find that the filling has just begun to melt at that point. The Twinkies tend to float, so you may wish to hold them under the oil with a slotted spoon until they brown.

Remove from the oil and let them rest on paper towels for 5 minutes (the creamy filling can be extremely hot if eaten immediately). Place the Twinkies on a warmed plate, drizzle the plate with fruit sauce, and sprinkle with the confectioners' sugar. Oh yeah, remove the sticks now!

SERVES 4

Fruit Sauce

- 1 cup chopped dried apricots
- 1 cup raspberries
- 1 tablespoon lemon juice
- ¼ cup fruity dessert wine (pear, apricot, or other favorite)
- 2 cups confectioners' sugar

Put all the ingredients into a medium saucepan on medium heat and cook until it boils. Take the pan off the heat and pour the fruit mixture into a small bowl, and cool until it reaches room temperature. Pour the cooled mixture into a blender or food processor and process until it is smooth, 1 to 2 minutes. If you wish, you may then run the mixture through a sieve to remove the seeds. Otherwise drizzle the sauce on the plates around the Twinkies.

MAKES 1½ TO 2 CUPS

FRIED OREO COOKIES

YOU WILL NOT BELIEVE HOW GOOD THESE TASTE! EVEN FOLKS WHO WOULD RATHER DIE THAN EAT ANYTHING FRIED, AND WHO DISDAIN THE VERY THOUGHT OF A COOKIE WHOSE FILLING IS ALLEGED TO CONTAIN NOTHING BUT SHORTENING AND SUGAR, RAVE ABOUT THE TASTE OF THESE LITTLE BUGGERS.

2 cups Hungry Jack pancake mix

1½ cups milk

2 eggs, beaten

4 teaspoons vegetable oil

1 large bag Oreo cookies

Oil for frying

Preheat the oil in a deep fryer to 385 degrees F.

In a wide, flat bowl, combine the pancake mix, milk, eggs, and vegetable oil. Whisk until the batter is smooth and free of lumps. Dip the Oreo cookies into the batter, making sure both sides are covered.

Slip the Oreos into the oil in small batches so that you leave space for them to fry. Cook until both sides are golden brown, 1 to 2 minutes, flipping them at least once. Remove with a slotted spoon and drain briefly on paper towels. Repeat with the rest of the Oreos to your heart's (or stomach's) content. Serve while still hot.

SERVES 54 (1 COOKIE EACH) OR 27 (2 COOKIES EACH) OR 13.5 (4 COOKIES EACH)

You get the picture . . .

AND, OH YES, WE MUSN'T FORGET THE . . .

DEEP-FRIED MILKY WAY BARS

THIS DESSERT WAS INVENTED IN, OF ALL PLACES, SCOTLAND. YOU'LL NEED POPSICLE STICKS TO COOK THESE PUPPIES.

1 cup flour

1 tablespoon sugar

1 egg, beaten

1 tablespoon melted butter

Pinch of salt

½ cup beer or milk, very cold

4 Milky Way (or Mars) Bars (see Note)

Oil for frying

In a large, deep bowl, combine the flour, sugar, egg, butter, salt, and cold beer and mix well with a whisk or hand mixer. Beat until the batter is smooth. Cover the bowl and refrigerate for 2 hours.

Push a Popsicle stick about one-third of the way into one end of each of the chocolate bars. Refrigerate the bars along with the batter for the remaining part of the 2 hours.

After about 1½ hours, preheat the oil in a deep fryer or Dutch oven to 385 degrees F.

Using the Popsicle stick as a handle, dip the bars one at a time into the chilled batter until they are completely covered. Drain briefly and then slip them into the hot oil to fry until the batter is golden brown, 1 to 2 minutes. Turn so both sides are golden. *Do not hold onto the stick while frying*—you will get burned with hot splattered oil. Also the stick itself will get very hot and can burn you.

Remove the bars from the oil with a slotted spoon, drain briefly on paper towels, then gobble them up. Be careful, as the interior of the bar can become molten caramel that will fry the inside of your mouth.

SERVES 4

Note: Snickers, Almond Joy, Twix, and Kit Kat bars will also work. Peanut butter cups and peppermint patties don't do well at all.

OREOS, TWINKIES, AND MILKY WAYS

AN EXCELLENT SOURCE OF FAT, SUGAR, AND CALORIES.

"Oh! A kid'll eat the middle of an Oreo first . . ." —Oreo slogan

"A big delight in every bite." —Twinkie slogan

"So light and fluffy it won't fill you up." —Milky Way slogan

- Nabisco has produced 490 billion Oreo cookies since its humble beginnings in 1912. If placed in a pile, these cookies would reach to the moon and back six times, or circle the earth at the equator 516 times. And on the Nabisco website you can play Oreo Adventure (and over 100 other real games)! Check it out at www.nabiscoworld.com.

- When you get intense hunger pangs and want something different, go to Twinkies' other website at www.twinkies.com and try out the Ho-Ho, Twinkie, or Ding Dong "recipe of the month."

- If you have nothing to do some lonely Saturday night, go to www.snickers.com and play a spirited round of Hunger Attack, the Game. Or you can sign up for Snickers' E-mail and join their newsletter list to receive the latest information on the bar and what's happening with their other products. What fun!

- The center of a Milky Way bar is nougat, which is made by whipping egg whites until they are light and frothy. Sugar syrup is then added, stabilizing the foam and creating a "frappe." A number of other flavoring ingredients are then added to the frappe. For more information on the history of Milky Way, see www.milkywaybar.com.

- If you count 50 calories for the Twinkie and 275 for the batter and oil, downing a fried Twinkie ain't that bad. Total damage: 425 calories, about the same as a slice of cherry pie à la mode.

- Milky Way bars were originally marketed in 1923 as "a chocolate malted drink in a candy bar."

- The deep-fried Mars Bar (or Milky Way) is thought to have originated in the town of Stonehaven in northeast Scotland. Its existence may help account for the fact that parts of Scotland have the highest incidence of heart disease, cancer, and stroke, the worst teeth, and the lowest life expectancy in the developed world.

BATTER UP!

Here are four batters for deep-frying fish, fruit, poultry, and meat. See the chart on page 6 for a sampling of frying times and temperatures to use for each of the battered foods.

BRINY BEER BATTER

AS YOU CAN SEE, I'VE LEFT THE CHART ON PAGE 7 VERY GENERIC; BECAUSE THE COOKING TIME AND TEMPERATURE ARE BASICALLY THE SAME FOR ALL FISH, DEPENDING ON IF THEY ARE FRESH OR FROZEN, YOU CAN TRY ALL DIFFERENT TYPES. I THINK YOU'LL FIND THEY'RE ALL DELICIOUS!

1 cup cornstarch

2 cups flour

1 tablespoon garlic powder

1 tablespoon green onion powder

1 tablespoon lemon granules (or zest)

1 tablespoon lemon (or citrus) pepper

1 tablespoon coarse salt

1 bottle or can of your favorite beer

In a large bowl, mix together all the ingredients (except 1 cup of the flour) and whisk until fully combined. Chill in the refrigerator for 20 minutes.

Pour the remaining cup of flour into a wide, shallow bowl and dredge the fish in the flour. Dip fish fillets or steaks into the batter mix and let the excess drip back into the bowl. Fry and enjoy.

SWEET MARY'S FRUIT BATTER

I'VE INCLUDED A FEW TYPES OF FRUIT IN THE CHART ON PAGE 7, BUT FEEL FREE TO EXPERIMENT. ALMOST ALL FRUITS REQUIRE THE SAME AMOUNT OF TIME IN THE FRYER: A QUICK 30 SECONDS, 1 MINUTE TOPS. CERTAIN SOFT, CUT FRUITS, SUCH AS BANANAS AND PINEAPPLES, DON'T FRY AS WELL, HOWEVER.

2 large eggs

1 tablespoon vegetable oil

½ cup buttermilk

2 tablespoons heavy cream

2 cups flour

¼ cup sugar

1 teaspoon baking powder

1 teaspoon salt

1 teaspoon vanilla extract

In a large bowl, mix together all the ingredients (except 1 cup of the flour) and whisk until the batter is smooth. Set aside in the refrigerator for 20 minutes to set.

Pour the remaining cup of flour into a shallow dish and dredge fruit pieces in it. Dip the floured fruit into the batter mix and let the excess drain back into the bowl. Fry and enjoy.

BIRD FRYIN' BEER BATTER

2½ cups flour

1 teaspoon cornstarch

1 tablespoon paprika

1 teaspoon onion powder

1 teaspoon salt

½ teaspoon pepper

1 bottle or can of your favorite beer

Sift 1½ cups of the flour, the cornstarch, paprika, onion powder, salt, and pepper into a wide, flat bowl. Add the beer, stirring with a wire whisk until well mixed, frothy, and smooth. Refrigerate the batter for 30 minutes. Just before using, whisk the batter once more to make sure it is well incorporated.

Pour the remaining cup of flour into a shallow dish and dredge chicken pieces in it. Dip them into the batter mix and let the excess drip back into the bowl. Deep fry and enjoy.

NACOGDOCHES STEAK DIP

ANY CUT OF STEAK OR ANY FILLET THAT'S ½ TO 1 INCH REQUIRES ABOUT 2½ TO 3 MINUTES IN A FRYER AT 350 DEGREES F FOR MEDIUM-RARE. THIS DIP IS DELICIOUS NO MATTER WHAT PART OF THE COW YOU USE (WELL, ALMOST!).

2 cups flour

½ cup cornstarch

1 teaspoon oregano

1 teaspoon chili powder

1 teaspoon baking powder

1 teaspoon powdered garlic

1 cup cold water

1 tablespoon vegetable (or olive) oil

Place all the dry ingredients (except 1 cup of the flour) into a wide, flat bowl and mix well. Add the water and oil and stir until thoroughly mixed. The batter should be quite thick.

Pour the remaining cup of flour into a shallow dish and dredge steaks or fillets in it. Dip them into the batter mix and let the excess drip back into the bowl. Deep-fry and enjoy.

CONVERSION CHARTS (APPROXIMATE)

U.S.	Metric
¼ teaspoon	1 ml
½ teaspoon	2 ml
1 teaspoon	5 ml
1 tablespoon	15 ml
¼ cup	50 ml
⅓ cup	75 ml
½ cup	125 ml
⅔ cup	150 ml
¾ cup	175 ml
1 cup	250 ml
1 quart	1 liter

WEIGHT

U.S.	Metric
1 ounce	30 grams
2 ounces	55 grams
3 ounces	85 grams
4 ounces	115 grams
8 ounces	225 grams
16 ounces	455 grams

TEMPERATURES

Fahrenheit	Celsius
32°	0°
212°	100°
250°	120°
275°	140°
300°	150°
325°	160°
350°	180°
375°	190°
400°	200°
425°	220°
450°	230°
475°	240°
500°	260°

THE REAL CONVERSION CHART

Located on the Diamond Bar (Calif.) High School website http://dbhs.wvusd.k12.ca.us/ Humor/, designed by chemistry teacher John Park and the "Chem team."

10^{12} microphones = 1 megaphone

10^6 bicycles = 2 megacycles

2000 mockingbirds = 2 kilomockingbirds

10 cards = 1 decacards

½ lavatory = 1 demijohn

10^6 fish = 1 microfiche

454 graham crackers = 1 pound cake

10^{12} pins = 1 terrapin

10 bowling pins = a strike

10^{21} picolos = 10^9 los = 1 gigolo

10 rations = 1 decoration

100 rations = 1 C-ration

10 millipedes = 1 centipede

3⅓ tridents =1 decadent, or one large mouthful of gum

5 dialogues = 1 decalogue

4 travels = 1 travelogue

4 grammys = 1 gramophone, or 4 gold records

8 nickels = 2 paradigms

2 snake eyes = 1 paradise

1 drake and 1 hen = 1 paradox

10^2 mental = 1 centimental

10 ornis = 5 ornamentals

10^1 mate = 1 decimate

10^{12} bulls = 1 terabull

10^{12} boos = 1 picoboo

OUR HUMBLE THANKS

THE FREQUENT FRYER FLYIN' FICKLE FINGER OF FÊTE AWARDS (AND MY HUMBLE THANKS) GO TO:

Sur la Table, Portland, Oregon

Lawrence Baab, Igloo Products

Rodney Barbour, Bayou Classic

Mark Carter, Simple Green

Robert Schwing, Char-Broil

Linda Myers, MyComm

John Davis

Milan Chuckovich

Pat and Tara Bennet

Patty Boday, Oregon Spice

Jeff Tracy

Brian Coleman, Char-Broil

Grigory Zaychick

Martha Barrows Dauber, Wells Lamont

John Suttner, Wells Lamont

Michael Armstrong, Swine & Dine

Patrick S. Terveer, Georgie Boy

Rich Allen, Georgie Boy

Tamara Meyer, APT

Linda Lutes

Loretta Barrett Oden, Corn Dance Cafe

Charles Charbonneau

Jim Kurfurst, Butcher Boys

Ken Haviland, Real Canadian Bacon Co.

Jeffery Hasseler, Ryan Artists

Rachel Ryan, Ryan Management

Aliza Fogelson

Angelica Canales

Judith Regan

Mike Starks, Soha Sign

Misty River

Carolyn Wells

Ardie Johnson

Paul Kirk

Smokey Hale

John Willingham

David Klose

The Car Dogs: Jack Rogers and Jim Minion

Amy Anderson and Mad Momma

Jon and Jana Trueb

Rocky Danner, National Barbecue News

Garry Howard, The Smoke Ring

Randall Oliver, Smart & Final

newbookscheap.com

Chris Sandberg, Have Smoke Will Travel

Chef Jamie Gwen

Cody Oliveira

Barry Pelts, Corky's

Michael R. Parr

Rubie Lloyd, Chefwear

Michelle Rosa, Chefwear

Carl Raymond

Kathy Browne

Chris Browne

Kara Browne

Tricia Browne

Tom Ryll

Barbara Johnson

Nathan Wu

Brea Lang

Scott Keegel

Steve Lane

Steven Sage, Brawny

Barry Nichols

RECIPE INDEX